Smuggled Stories
from the Holy Land

Carmen Taha Jarrah

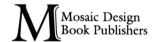
Mosaic Design
Book Publishers

Smuggled Stories from the Holy Land
by Carmen Taha Jarrah

Copyright © 2015 Carmen Taha Jarrah
ALL RIGHTS RESERVED

First Printing – March 2015
ISBN: 978-0-9961106-0-0 (PB)
ISBN: 978-0-9961106-1-7 (eBook)
Library of Congress Control Number: 2015934147

All photos copyright by Carmen Taha Jarrah.
Cover photo courtesy of Steve Ghannam.
Cover design and text formatting by Mosaic Design Book Publishers.
Author photo by Michael Kakoullis.

Printed in the United States of America on acid-free paper

Published by Mosaic Design Book Publishers
www.mosaicdesignbookpublishers.com
Dearborn, Michigan USA

For Jumana, Janan and Anwar, my children

And, for the brilliant and beautiful Aya Abuelaish, a 13-year-old girl, a poet, who aspired to become a journalist, but never had the chance. She was killed by the Israeli army on January 16, 2009, at her home in the Gaza Strip, along with her two sisters and a cousin. Perhaps the stories in this book are the kind she would have reported. This humble offering is in her name.

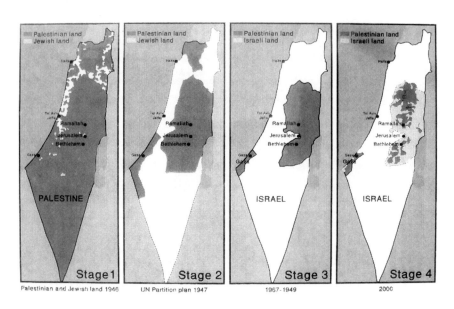

Map posted in the courtyard outside the Church of the Nativity in Bethlehem

Table of Contents

Preface

NOW THAT I HAVE SEEN, I AM RESPONSIBLE.

This line of graffiti on the Israeli-built separation wall in the Holy Land is my motivation for this book.

I have had the privilege of travelling widely throughout Israel and the Occupied Palestinian Territories. In 2009, I journeyed with eight other members of the Arab Jewish Women's Peace Coalition from Edmonton, Alberta. I volunteered in 2010 to help Palestinians pick their olives in the Bethlehem District, where I joined about 100 other peace activists from around the world. The following year, I participated in the Path of Abraham tour with a first-of-its-kind Canadian interfaith group comprised of Jews, Christians and Muslims. Together we made a pilgrimage of sorts to our respective holy sites, sharing in each other's religious rituals and traditions: praying at the Western Wall on the Sabbath, attending a Christian service in the Garden of Gethsemane and communal prayers at the Al-Aqsa mosque.

I walked along "sterilized" streets, ancient streets and Jewish-only streets, explored olden medinas and the ramparts of the Old City of Jerusalem. I experienced military checkpoints and the Wall up close, the ghettoes and virtual open-air prisons left in their wake. I saw confiscated Palestinian hilltops, demolished homes and uprooted olive groves. I witnessed the lack of freedoms and daily humiliations. Hopefulness and hopelessness round every corner. I saw ancient ruins and ruined lives and antiquity and modernity existing side-by-side.

I wrote this book because the Palestinian narrative is largely missing from mainstream media reports. I wanted to do my part by raising greater awareness of what I witnessed and by imparting some of the stories I heard from displaced and dispossessed Palestinians, to tell of their continued suffering under Israel's decades-long military occupation and colonization campaign. I also wanted to pass along some of the stories I heard from extraordinary Israelis and Palestinians, peacemakers, true heroes, who rarely make mainstream news, stories of resistance and resilience, stories of remorse and redemption. I vowed their stories would not atrophy into oblivion; my notebooks and journal would not sit on some shelf collecting dust. Their stories would not be forgotten.

This book is a compilation of some of the stories I heard; I changed many of the names to ensure people's privacy and for some, their safety, and maintained the names of non-anonymous individuals. It is based primarily on copious notes I took of observations and personal testimonies, which I translated and quoted to the best of my ability, including transcribed audio recordings of some of the meetings and presentations. I also relied on information provided by alternative tour guides, families I stayed with and material provided by members of the various organizations I met daily: brochures, books and maps. I documented what the Occupation looks like by taking thousands of photographs. The Holy Land is haemorrhaging, and I feel responsible to tell others.

This book is not an academic dissertation or historical chronicle about the "conflict" between Israelis and Palestinians. I do not consider myself an authority even though I have read many books.

A Palestinian poet, who goes by the pen name, Nahida in Exile, said it best in her poem:

I want to tell the world a story
About a home with a broken lantern
And a burnt doll
About a picnic that wasn't enjoyed
About an axe that killed a tulip
A story about a fire that consumed a plait
A story about a tear that couldn't run down
I want to tell a story about a goat that wasn't milked
About a mother's dough that wasn't baked
About a wedding that wasn't celebrated
And a baby girl that didn't grow up
About a football that wasn't kicked
About a dove that didn't fly
I want to tell a story about a key that wasn't used
About a classroom that wasn't attended
About a playground that was silenced
About a book that wasn't read
About a besieged lonely farm
And about its fruits that weren't picked
About a lie that wasn't discovered
A story about a church that's no longer prayed in
And a mosque that no longer stands
And a culture no longer rejoiced
I want to tell a story about a muddy grassy roof
About a stone that faced a tank
And about a stubborn flag that refuses to lie down
About a spirit that cannot be defeated
I want to tell the world a story.

Part One

ONE

Oasis of Peace

There really can be no peace without justice. There can be no justice without truth. And there can be no truth, unless someone rises up to tell you the truth.

Louis Farrakhan

My someday is here…

It is 4:00 PM, October 18, 2009. Legs wobbly after the 11-hour flight from Toronto, I pull my carry-on bag behind me, following the stream of people down a series of ramps inside the shiny arrivals terminal at Ben Gurion airport near Tel Aviv. I end up in a large, crowded room; people are lined up in front of a row of kiosks waiting to go through immigration. To my right, a separate area is marked for Israeli citizens. I stand at the end of one of several lines for visitors, filled with a mixture of fear and euphoria.

A young Israeli woman at the counter reaches for my passport. I hold my breath as she scrutinizes it, praying she will allow me through. I've heard about the delays, searches, detentions and deportations some people face trying to gain entry into Israel, especially if one's surname is Arabic, like mine.

"Why are you here?" she asks. She is poker-faced, but speaks in a polite tone.

"I'm here on vacation." I smile, hoping the answer will suffice, and remind myself, if she presses for specifics, "Do not slip and mention Palestine or the Occupied Palestinian Territories."

To my surprise she stamps my passport and hands it back to me, already stretching her neck past me and addressing the next person in line. I step to the side, waiting for the other four members of the Arab-Jewish Women's Peace Coalition to be processed. Relieved and grateful, I tuck my passport inside my bag and turn to face the lines of people, watching as they inch forward intermittently towards the row of kiosks, tugging their bags, yawning and shifting their weight from one leg to the other. Above the din of jumbled voices and shuffling feet, I hear the sporadic clicks as passports are stamped. Little do I know what impact the precious entry stamp will have on me and the doors it has just opened into an amazing journey in search of peace, in a place where the notion is seemingly empty rhetoric, a cliché. I feel blessed to be standing in the Holy Land, about to burst from excitement at the potential learning, knowing the entry stamp will allow me to see ancient places for the first time and meet peacemakers from both sides of the "conflict," Israelis and Palestinians. I sense the stamp will test my assumptions, that I will never be the same again.

The last woman in our peace coalition clears immigration without delay. The air outside is hot and heavy as we board a waiting van outside the terminal. A half-hour later, our driver exits the main highway and follows a winding, gravel road up a slope to the village of Neve Shalom/Wahat al-Salaam; the Hebrew and Arabic names, respectfully, translate to Oasis of Peace. The village is located halfway between Jerusalem and Tel Aviv. It is already dark by now. I cannot see much, except for blackened hillsides freckled with lights. I check in at the village's two-story administration building, looking forward to much-needed sleep as I drag my suitcase along a lit path leading to rows of uniform guest houses that hug the undulating slope.

At dawn a rooster crows, sounding as if he has laryngitis. I tiptoe quietly across the room hoping not to wake my roommate, open the back door of my guesthouse and step outside onto a small patio. I stretch and inhale the fresh morning air. I gaze out at the pastoral panorama before me, a valley of rectangular fields of green and yellow, a patchwork quilt, and beyond them through the gossamer haze along the horizon, the rocky hills have been planted with rows of spruce, olive and other fruit trees. I run my finger over the small patio table, leaving a track in the fine layer of dust, needing to feel something tactile to prove that I am really here.

Established in the early 1970s, I only recently learned about this village during our group's planning meetings. The Oasis of Peace is a paradigm for the possibility of peaceful coexistence between two supposed enemies. Sitting on a hilltop, its modest homes are shaded by orange and almond trees, grapevines, evergreens and flowering shrubs. There are several rows of guest houses for visitors and tourists, conference facilities where Arab-Jewish seminars are held, a School for Peace, a spiritual center and a white dome-shaped structure for meditation called the House of Silence, which we plan on visiting at some point during our two-week stay.

The rooster crows again, breaking the quietness. My eyes follow the sound to the bottom of the slope, hidden by trees. Birds begin chirping and flitting about. I think about how serendipitous it is that I would join a women's peace group in Edmonton and now have the opportunity to come here and experience life in a one-of-a-kind village where Palestinians and Jews *choose* to live together in harmony.

Only two years ago, I stood on a hilltop in southern Lebanon overlooking the border with Israel, gazing down at the beige landscape on the Lebanese side of the boundary and the green hills on the Israeli side. I recall seeing a sign written in Arabic, which read, *Falastine*, Palestine, and dreaming of one day visiting.

At breakfast, just as I have since childhood, I tear off a piece of pita bread, pinch its sides into a scoop, dip it into the dollop of *labnee* on my plate and top it with a black olive before popping it into my mouth. I relish the familiar tang of the creamy yoghurt cheese mixed with the slight bitterness of the olive, and listen to the women at the table around me discussing what to do with our free day. The remaining women in our peace coalition are scheduled to arrive later this evening.

"How about we go to Jaffa?" Shai suggests.

Of course, I'm thrilled. Who wouldn't want to visit one of the world's most continuously inhabited cities?

"I'm in! I want to see it all, every corner of the Holy Land," I pipe up in between mouthfuls. "It matters little to me where I start the voyage."

I read about the Old Jaffa, located on a hill overlooking the Mediterranean Sea, its port is reportedly the oldest in the world and dates back to the Bronze Age, a place steeped in myths and legends. Its location is one of beauty and blight. Like many ancient cities in the Holy Land and elsewhere in the Middle East, it has been coveted and conquered by many over the millennia: the Canaanites, Philistines and Babylonians, Alexander the Great, King Richard the Lion Heart, Saladin and Napoleon, just to name some.

More recently, its predominately Arab population was driven out when the State of Israel was created in 1948. Jewish immigrants from around the world occupied some of the Palestinian homes, though many were damaged or destroyed in the violent conquest, or left to decay. Israeli authorities considered demolishing Old Jaffa, but instead restored it into an artist's colony to cater to tourism. A year later, Israel annexed Old Jaffa and its surroundings into the city of Tel Aviv, and today mainly Jewish people live here, mixed with fewer numbers of Palestinian Christians and Muslims.

Our driver drops our peace coalition off in Old Jaffa near Clock Tower Square, a prominent landmark built in 1906 by the Ottomans and once a commercial hub. We walk towards the sea, stopping along a road, the Sea Wall Promenade, which follows a restored, ancient sea wall. At the toe of the slope below me, several people are lying in the sun on a white beach. A bronzed woman lathers on sunscreen. Two men swim. A third man, hip deep in the water, flings a fishing rod. I look out at the undulating stretch of coastline and turquoise water, soothing like a mother's embrace. The child in me has the sudden urge to dash down the slope with carefree abandon, kick off my sandals and splash about in the cool water.

To the northeast, the white strip of beach stretches into the distance.

Modern block-style hotels and apartment buildings of Tel Aviv follow the sinuous shore. To the southwest, on a promontory rising some 40 metres above the sea, are the remnants of Old Jaffa. I see the white minaret of the century-old Mahmoudiyeh Mosque piercing the sky. My gaze drifts down the partially forested slope to the tiny Jama' al-Bahr, or Mosque of the Sea. It sits at the edge of the Sea Wall Promenade, which curves with the shore out of view, overlooking what survives of the ancient stone harbour, visible in the distance. I peer through the viewfinder of my camera at the mosque and snap several photographs.

I zoom in on the Mosque by the Sea with my telephoto lens for a closer view. The ochre-coloured structure looks ethereal, unadorned and forlorn. I sense this little mosque at the edge of the sea would be an extra-ordinary spot to supplicate, unlike any other mosque or place where I've prayed. I feel an affinity to it that I cannot explain. For a brief moment, I am part of the place and not simply a spectator.

I picture myself praying within its hushed interior at sunset. Alone. Standing on the edge of a worn prayer rug with my hands overlapped against my chest. A cool breeze blows in from an open seafront window, caresses my face. The salty breath of the sea mixed with the sweet scent of jasmine and frangipani floats in. Silently, I recite *surahs*, from the Holy Qur'an. Kneel and glorify God to the rhythm of the waves collapsing on the rocky shore. Prostrate and repeat three times: *Subhana Rabi Al-A'la*, Glory be to my Lord, the Most Sublime.

I focus my camera on the minaret. Near the top is a circular veranda. I imagine the *muezzins*, who stood there once, five times a day to recite the call to prayer. It is silent now. I've read it is no longer a functional mosque. I do not know how old it is, but the mosque is not likely old enough to have observed the comings and goings of the earliest conquerors that stormed ashore. However, I suspect it is old enough to have seen the expulsion of the indigenous Jewish population by the Turks during World War I, and decades later, it would have welcomed waves of Jewish immigrants from Europe to the new state while witnessing the exodus of Palestinians from Old Jaffa. In my mind's eye, I see the mosque, a helpless sentinel, watching crowds of men, women and children as they clambered onto boats carrying what they can of their possessions, their frightened faces staring back and slowly fading into history, hoping one day to return home, not knowing that they never will.

As if waking from a dream, I am suddenly aware of the mirth and chatter of my Jewish and Arab sisters beside me, and wonder if they know that my mind had drifted to a moment of timelessness. I lost myself in the past, lost myself in a lost world. I close my eyes and inhale the dank smell of the sea as if I can never be satiated, savour it, try to capture it as if in a bottle to take back with me. I want the moment to last, but we are moving on.

We head west along Roslan Street towards Old Jaffa, passing Jaffa Museum and the Arab-Hebrew Theater, and continue until Roslan Street turns into Mifratz Shlomo Street. We walk towards Slope Park, past a Napoleon cannon, and St. Peter Church, which was constructed on top of the ruins of a crusader fort. Buried under the fort is a Byzantine church. I marvel at what might be buried under the church, for only when exhumed will the earth cede more of its secrets.

Jaffa's ancient people and numerous conquerors have all left their mark in the strata beneath my feet. It is sobering to be literally walking on layers and layers of antiquity. The weight of Jaffa's history is palpable as we continue along the serpentine cobblestone pathways of the old quarter. Little remains of Jaffa's former Arab character. It now has the artsy air of a tourist town. I am surprised few people are out and about. Aged stone buildings inset with stone arches above windows and doorways, shells of their former selves, have been restored and converted into museums, antique stores, art galleries and studios, shops and restaurants, the old and the new, side-by-side existing symbiotically. I step into a few shops. On the inside, they have the feel and look of trendy boutiques, reminding me of the over-priced shops in Banff, Alberta, that cater to tourists. Contemporary artwork and modern shelving stocked with colourful ceramics, jewelry and souvenirs mask the history of Old Jaffa.

After walking around for a couple of hours, we stop for something to drink at Yamit Restaurant, sit in an outdoor patio overlooking a beautiful view of the sea and remnants of the ancient stone harbour jutting into the water, enjoying ourselves, feeding off one another's excitement, chatting and giggling like a group of closely knit school girls, even though we are all over 50 years old, and one of the sisters is over 80.

Later that evening, the remaining women in our coalition arrive. We gather in a conference hall back at the Oasis of Peace, where we sit in a large circle to receive an orientation session from village officials. Another group, which calls itself Pilgrims for Ibillin, comprised of about 20 men and women of various ages from the United States, is also here. Rita, a cheerful Palestinian, who works for the village's communication and development department, welcomes us and facilitates the introductions.

Alimah, an Arab sister and one of our founding members of the Arab-Jewish Women's Peace Coalition, provides the background about our group and purpose of our journey.

"Our group formed in 1991 after the first Gulf War," she begins. "Several Jewish and Arab activists met at a peace vigil in Edmonton. We realized we had a lot more to talk about than our anti-war activism. In the first year, we met weekly to dialogue issues surrounding the Middle East, divisive issues that were near and dear to our hearts.

"Slowly over the years we sort of unpacked and unwound some of those issues and eventually came to a place where we could meet once a month. And that's where we're at now. We try to deepen our understanding of one another. We go out to talk to other groups and tell our story, always together, an Arab and a Jew."

Alimah mentions that there are currently about 20 members in our peace coalition, although only nine of us have come on this peace journey. Some of the women have been to the Holy Land before, but saw only a piece of it; for others, it is our first time.

"We always wanted to come here and meet other people who are doing similar work and our dream has come true," she finishes up, flashing a smile as she looks around at the group. A few members of the Pilgrims for Ibillin nod their heads, as if in appreciation.

Doreet, a small-framed Jewish lady who works as an educator, briefs us about the village and its unique School for Peace.

"There are currently 54 families living in the Oasis of Peace. Half are Palestinian, half are Jewish," she tells us in a quiet tone. "The goal is for both sides to live together on equal grounds. The Oasis of Peace is like a cooperative. People do not own the land. There used to be nothing on this hill. It was donated by the church.

"Israel does not confiscate land from a church, only from Palestinians," she adds without humour.

The late Father Bruno Hussar, a Dominican priest who converted to Christianity from Judaism, donated the land to build the village and had the vision to create a place where people of different faiths and ethnicities could live together in peace. He was inspired by the Old Testament, namely chapter 32:18 of the Book of Isaiah, which says, "My people shall dwell in an oasis of peace." Hence, too, the name of the village. There is a waiting list of Jews and Arabs wanting to move here, and village officials plan to expand the village to house about 150 families.

"It's about recognition and respect," Doreet tells a rapt audience. "We need to live together, Arabs and Jews."

At this I feel like singing *Halleluiah* at the top of my voice.

"Here, kids are not racists, but on the outside it is different. Our elementary school has no map. It is the only bilingual, bi-ethnic school in Israel, but it needs funding since we get no financial support like other schools in Israel. We raise funds for education and are now beginning to receive support from organizations in Europe and North America."

An elderly man across the room asks, "How are residents of the village viewed by other Israelis, both Arab and Jewish Israelis?"

"Jews think we are naïve, insignificant," Doreet replies. "They can go on with their lives without paying attention, in denial of history. There is so much segregation. For Arabs, the reality is awful."

She also talks about the village's School for Peace, an internationally renowned educational centre that conducts research and collaborates with universities in Israel to offer a variety of courses. Here, experienced educators and facilitators provide inter-group encounters and have hosted more than 45,000 youth and adults. These encounters create opportunities for dialogue, to hear each other's opinions and emotions and to help each participant understand their individual role in the "conflict." The School for Peace also trains facilitators in conflict management. I am inspired and fascinated by the idea of a school dedicated to building peace. God knows the world needs more of them. Questions flit through my mind. But my thoughts are scattered, so I do not ask.

Hours later, I am still wide awake, lying in bed in the dark, my brain in overdrive. The day's lessons and adventure play back. I can't process it all.

How do I feel?

I am anxious to take it all in, peel away the layers of truth. I lift my head off an overstuffed pillow, punch it a few times, trying to get more comfortable, thinking how this land, ancient Palestine, feels like the *watan*, Lebanon, my ancestral homeland, only a few hundred kilometres north of here. What I have witnessed so far feels familiar, like home even though I have never been here before. The climate and the rolling topography, terraced with olive groves and grapevines and diversity of fruit trees are not unlike the hills of Lebanon, or Syria or Jordan. The foods, the language and traditions are familiar. I look like I belong, like the locals, Jewish *and* Palestinian. I smile to myself, remembering one of the shop owners in Old Jaffa, who sold antique keys and assumed I could understand when he spoke to me in Hebrew.

My arm numbs up, forcing me to roll to my other side. My thoughts drift to tomorrow, when the journey officially begins in another ancient city, Jerusalem. I will see for myself the impact of Israel's military occupation and confiscation practices in the Palestinian territories, what non-violent resistance and perseverance look like, how Jews and Palestinians live in the Holy Land, another reality entirely.

TWO

The Great Act of Taking

We'll make a pastrami sandwich of them. We'll insert a strip of Jewish settlement, in between the Palestinians, then another strip of Jewish settlement, right across the West Bank, so that in 25 years time, neither the United Nations, nor the United States, nobody, will be able to tear it apart.

Ariel Sharon to Winston Churchill III, Journalist, 1973

I am in a second-floor office on Ben Yehuda Street in West Jerusalem, helping myself to the various free booklets. I leaf through one titled, "So What Should We Do?" before the start of our tour of the Jerusalem district. This tour is not the regular tourist type. It is provided by the Israeli Committee Against House Demolitions (ICAHD), a non-profit, non-violent grassroots organization established in 1997 by a group of Israeli Jews. ICAHD focuses on Israel's demolition of Palestinian homes: blocking bulldozers sent to demolish these houses, raising awareness and mobilizing people from around the world, raising funds and rebuilding demolished homes.

Yahav, a Jewish Israeli and volunteer with ICAHD, will be our guide. He appears to be in his twenties, with black hair and beard and striking blue-green eyes. He and the nine of us women, five Jews and four Arabs, sit in a circle. The modest office is bright. Shelves of educational material and maps line the walls.

"I am going to give you a hundred years of history of Israel and Palestine in 18 minutes," he promises, which makes some of us chuckle.

As he speaks, he takes turns making eye contact with each of us, explaining that in 1917 Britain conquered Palestine from the Ottoman Empire and issued the Balfour Declaration for the creation of a Jewish homeland in Palestine. Jews began moving Palestinians off the land by buying up property from wealthy Arabs. Jewish immigration continued and spiked following the Holocaust, causing violent clashes between the indigenous Palestinians and armed Zionist militias opposed to Britain's restrictions on immigration.

"In time, Britain essentially gave up and left. There was no oil here. No diamonds," Yahav says. "They told the UN to do something about it. The map makers knew it wouldn't work."

The UN divided Palestine, giving 54 percent to the Jews, even though they only owned six percent of the land, and allocating 46 percent to the Palestinians, who owned 93 percent of Palestine. The Palestinians naturally objected. War broke out. On May 15, 1948, Zionist militias declared Palestine as the State of Israel; it became Independence Day for Israelis and the *Nakba* (Catastrophe) for Palestinians.

Israel depopulated and destroyed 418 Palestinian villages. Over 750,000 Palestinians became refugees, fleeing to the West Bank and Gaza, or to neighbouring Lebanon, Syria, Jordan and elsewhere. Israel then closed its borders and enacted laws to prevent Palestinian refugees from returning. Some Palestinians stayed and today they number almost two million. They have become de-facto Israeli citizens.

"In 1967, Israel grabbed more Palestinian territory and, in the process, two million Palestinians." Yahav continues.

"Israel said, 'We want the land, but not the people.'"

Looking right at me, and with calmness in his voice, he says, "I call it The Great Act of Taking."

He has that young-hip-professorial look to him. I am curious to know if his parents approve of his work with ICAHD, providing the Palestinian narrative surrounding the history of this sacred space, chipping away at the walls of misinformation built by corporate media and his open criticism of Israeli policy. I glance around the room, also wondering what my Jewish sisters are thinking.

It is sad and strange for me. We came all this way as a peace coalition, but do not have a common understanding of the historical and current "conflict." We do not agree on what to call the Wall or what to call Israel's policies and practices in the Occupied Palestinian Territories. We do not even have a mutual understanding between the Arab women themselves and the Jewish women themselves. I continue to be nagged by questions. Is it necessary to have agreement on at least the fundamentals of the conflict, given that dialogue is the main focus of our coalition? How different would our peace coalition be if there was consensus? Am I being too idealistic or naive in believing there should be common ground? Regardless, we are all here, a sister-hood of peace activists committed to similar values. I remind myself to keep an open heart and mind, knowing from experience, and my mother hammering it in my head, not to be too confident or complacent in what I think I know. Moreover, I do not even know how much I do not know.

"Our driver is waiting out front," Yahav says, rising to his feet.

We follow him down the stairs and board a mini-bus. The driver takes us through West Jerusalem: a modern, clean, and green metropolis. We get off the bus and walk 50 metres to an observation point on a hilltop, with a panoramic view of the valleys and hills southeast of Jerusalem. On the top of a ridge, kilometres away, I see an illegal settlement for Jewish people. The dense rows of identical, white stone apartments, condos and houses stand out on the landscape, contrasting the Palestinian neighbourhoods, which are not as closely packed and whose older-looking homes appear organic and blend into the rocky hills.

And then I see it, through the haze. The massive cement wall is menacing even from a distance. It snakes along ridges, up and down slopes, encircling homes, bends and dips out of view. It follows winding roads, turning some of them into dead ends. Using my telephoto lens as binoculars, I zoom in on one section of the Wall that has trapped a two-story house perched on the edge of a steep, rock-face slope, splitting it from the rest of the Palestinian community. I've known about the Wall, but for me, seeing it is not only believing, but also never forgetting. I cannot imagine how the Palestinians must feel being walled in, their lives literally stonewalled. I am roused from my thoughts by a nearby conversation.

"Israel is not slowing down," Yahav is saying. "The number of illegal settlements has doubled since the Oslo peace talks."

"Are two states possible?" one of the women in our coalition asks.

"Yes, if Israel withdraws to the Green Line," he replies.

I turn my attention to the west and see the ancient walls of *Haram Al-Sharif*, the Noble Sanctuary, or Temple Mount as some prefer to call it, distinguishable by the Dome of the Rock glistening like a jewel on the opposite ridge, iconic of the Jerusalem skyline. It has pulled at me and intrigued me since childhood — a wall tapestry depicting the Dome of the Rock hung in my parent's living room for years. It topped my list of places to visit, and here I am observing it for the first time. I can feel its energy from where I am standing. I want to experience it up close. I take a panoramic photograph to show my brother who visited Jerusalem and photographed the eastern hills from the same vantage point, before the settlements, before the Wall. I want to compare photographs when I return to Canada.

Back on board, our mini-bus winds its way east, towards the opposite ridge I just observed, down into the valley through a Palestinian neighbourhood. The road is narrow and potholed. It hurts to see groups of children playing amid piles of rubble and garbage. I snap photographs through the streaked window. Many of the children smile and wave as we drive by; some give the peace sign. I smile back, waving and making the peace sign, even though my heart aches for them.

"Palestinians pay 40 percent of the taxes, but receive only eight percent of the money for services," Yahav tells us.

Our driver stops near a large pile of rubble with chunks of cement and rebar sticking out.

"It is a demolished home," Yahav says. "The owner left it as it was when Israel destroyed it in 2006."

Israel has made it almost impossible for Palestinians to obtain permits to build on their own land, charging thousands of dollars only to have some bureaucrat deny a permit application on some bogus "technicality," forcing many, who need shelters for their growing families, to build without a permit and live under the daily threat of a demolition order. Yet, it is acceptable for Israel to confiscate and annex privately-owned, Palestinian lands and build settlements for Jewish immigrants from around the world.

"Look around you," he tells us, "Israelis and Palestinians continue to talk about how to share the pizza while Israel is eating the entire thing."

We reach a section of the three-story cement wall I saw from the opposite mountain ridge, cutting through and separating the Palestinian neighbourhood from Ma'ale Adumim. It is the largest settlement in the West Bank, an exclusively Jewish mini-city of about 40,000. Driving alongside the Wall, I feel as if I have suddenly shrunk as we follow a Jewish-only road running parallel to it, up the slope to the settlement. I lower my head to my lap, kink my neck up to see the top of the Wall.

Ma'ale Adumim is a green oasis in an otherwise dry rocky terrain. It's like I've discovered Shangri-La on a hilltop. At its entrance, the Fountain of Peace, with its two dove statues, greet us. The paved streets are clean, spacious and lined on both sides with palm trees and flowering shrubs.

"To feed their families, some Palestinians come here to work as street cleaners and gardeners," Yahav tells us.

I notice that few people are out and about. A couple dressed in western clothes ambles hand in hand. A young mother pushes a baby carriage along the adjacent walkway fronting a park embellished with ancient olive trees, perhaps thousands of years old. They appear out of place. I assume they were uprooted from elsewhere, likely Palestinian land, and transplanted here. I watch out the window as we drive past modern schools and sports facilities, art galleries and libraries.

"It's paid for largely by American taxpayers," Yahav points out. "You need to put pressure on your government to stop this."

He explains that Israel offers tax incentives for Jews living anywhere in the world to move to the Promised Land, zero percent mortgages, armed guards and gated green communities.

His words bring to mind numerous advertisements I have read on-line enticing Jewish people to make *Aliyah* to Israel. Interestingly, the word *Aliyah*, in both Arabic and Hebrew means "ascent." The term, however, refers to the immigration of Jewish people to the "Land of Israel." For some Jews, it is a tenant of Zionism. Other Jews, in particular right-wing settlers, believe they have a divinely-ordained right to return to the Promised Land. This right is enshrined in Israel's Law of Return and can be exercised by a Jewish person anywhere in the world, but the advertisements neglect to mention that making *Aliyah* means occupying stolen Palestinian lands.

We head west along a new highway towards the Palestinian village of Anata, located in the rocky hills north of Jerusalem. On a hillside, a Bedouin and his son guide their flock of sheep. Further on, we come to a patch of ground with rows of *things* poking out of the parched earth. When it registers, I gasp loudly, getting curious looks from the sisters sitting nearby. I am looking at rows of olive tree stumps about two feet high. Barely able to suppress my anger, I hide behind my camera and busy myself snapping photographs, shocked by the cruelty and criminality that I am witnessing. The destruction of olive trees, for many Palestinians, their only source of income, is standard practice for Israel.

The mini-bus lurches forward and squeaks as our driver manoeuvres around boulders and deep ruts, down a steep narrow road along the outskirts of Anata. There is little greenery to contrast the rocky terrain. On both sides of the pitted road, piles of jagged cement blocks, rubble and strewn garbage are interspersed with small homes, made mostly of corrugated metal roofs held down by big rocks and tires. Their sides are built from scrap siding, sheet metal and cardboard. A group of children playing with nothing, it seems, stop and stare as we lumber past.

Our ICAHD tour includes a luncheon with Salim Shawamreh at the Beit Arabiya Peace Center. Salim is standing outside waiting for us.

"Welcome. Welcome," he greets us warmly. Tall, he has curly salt-and-pepper hair and moustache, and wears glasses.

"*Marhaba*! I'm Carmen," I say, shaking his hand. "Thank you for having us."

As I wait for the women to finish their greetings, I take in the russet hills around me. Staring down at me, across the valley on a ridge above the peace center, is the Shin Bet Prison and interrogation building. It is difficult to miss. The Wall is also in full view further down the slope, running along a portion of the recently-built Eastern Ring Road that connects the new, illegal Jewish settlements, which Israel annexed to the Jerusalem district.

My eyes are drawn to a splash of colour on the peace center's exterior north wall: a large painting of a bulldozer rolling through a hilly landscape, flanked by protesters, with tanks and missiles on both sides. Two red lightning bolts strike the bulldozer from a blue cloud. Above the bulldozer, the spirits of two women float skywards, like angels. One is Rachel Corrie, an American peace activist who was killed by an Israeli driving a Caterpillar bulldozer as she stood in front of a Palestinian house, trying to defend it from demolition. The other is Nuha Sweiden, a pregnant Palestinian woman who was killed during a house demolition in Gaza.

I notice a small note in the bottom, right-hand corner of the painting and move in closer to read it. It says:

DONATED BY NORTH AMERICAN WORKERS AGAINST THE

U.S. OCCUPATION OF IRAQ AND THE ISRAELI OCCUPATION

OF PALESTINE — AUGUST — 2003

"Please come in," Salim tells us, after allowing some time for the women to look around. He gestures for us to follow him inside.

The interior of the peace center is one, big room with no inner walls. Red oriental rugs cover over half of the tiled floor. Rectangular foam mats encased in red fabric line the walls. It is cozy yet museum-like. Framed posters hang on the south wall — a documentary photo essay on house demolitions and Salim's ordeal. I linger for a while near the entrance, admiring the simplicity and power of a place dedicated to peace building. The other women approach a south wall and begin viewing the framed posters hanging on it, large photo collages titled:

THE DEMOLITION OF A HOME IS THE DEMOLITION OF A FAMILY.

REBUILDING AND REBUILDING THE HOUSE OF PEACE

Another poster shows a convoluted flow chart:

PROCESS FOR OBTAINING A BUILDING PERMIT

With its different coloured boxes and arrows in all directions, it reminds me of the flow charts I have had to prepare for various government processes during my career, some of which became too drawn-out and difficult to decipher.

I notice Salim's wife, Arabiya, after whom the center is named, busy chopping vegetables in the corner kitchen. She's petite and her pretty face is framed by a black *hijab*. I walk up to her and introduce myself. Seemingly lost in her own world, she musters a faint smile, sadness and tiredness ooze from her eyes. My mind goes blank. I do not have a single intelligent thing to say.

"It's a pleasure meeting you," I finally say and retreat to the opposite side of the room where I sit cross-legged on one of the foam mats covering the floor, feeling like an awkward teenager.

What can I say to her without sounding obtuse and insensitive? How are you? How's life been going for you?

As Salim begins his story, it is apparent he has done this many times before.

"On July 9, 1998, after four years of living in my new house, my family was eating lunch. We heard loud voices. Over 300 soldiers surrounded the house. They told us, 'You have 15 minutes to take your belongings,'" he says. "They beat me and arrested me. They forced my wife and seven children out with tear gas. My children were crying. My wife passed out. The neighbours came and tried to stop them. We tried to resist, but in the end they bulldozed my house.

"They also cut down 52 trees I had planted. The soldiers left nothing standing. CNN filmed it."

As he talks, I glance at Arabiya, her motions mechanical, carrying platters of food and stacks of plates and setting them on the table, her flip-flops slapping against her heels in the background.

"We lived in a tent while we rebuilt our house. Twenty-eight days after we finished, on August 3, 1998, at four in the morning, we woke up to machine guns pointed in our faces. Israeli soldiers forced us out and demolished our house. They told me that my permit application was missing two signatures.

"So, the next time I applied for a permit, I got 400 signatures from people who lived in Anata and had no objection and we rebuilt for the third time. Volunteers from around the world including Israelis and Palestinians helped."

Salim stops when he notices that Arabiya needs a hand, excuses himself and walks over to her. He lifts a large, red pot from the stove, sets it on the floor and removes its lid, replacing it with a face-down, stainless steel platter. Squeezing the two together tightly, he tips them over and raises the pot. The contents, moulded in the shape of the pot, are left on the platter, like an upside down cake. I know from the savoury aroma permeating the room and from Salim's tipping of the pot that we are going to be having *maqlouba* for lunch, rice with layers of chicken, fried eggplant, cauliflower and peppers. Arabiya squats on the floor, serving spoon in hand, partially hidden by clouds of steam as she shapes the contents into a small mountain.

I reflect on the name of this traditional dish, which means "topsy-turvy," a name encapsulating what Israel has turned Palestinian life into.

"Let's eat while the food is still hot," Salim says, transferring the steaming platter to the table. Like a typical Arab host, Arabiya has made enough food to feed three times the number of guests. The mountain of *maqlouba* in the center is surrounded with different types of salads and yogurt. I pile up my plate, take a seat on a foam mat and bite into my lunch. It is the best *maqlouba* I have ever tasted. I look around for Arabiya to compliment her, but she seems to have left.

Salim eats quickly and continues his story. On April 4, 2001, soldiers came with two bulldozers and demolished his house for the third time. I picture his children leaving for school that morning with their home intact and returning to a pile of rubble. His wife went into shock and his daughter went blind temporarily.

"Her sight returned," he says. "I told her not to be afraid, that I'd protect her. She said, 'How can you protect me from the soldiers?'"

One of the women sitting close to me tears up. I am speechless. I want to offer some comfort, but what relief can I possibly bring? Here, the boogeyman is real; it does not lurk under beds or inside closets. It barges into bedrooms at night, forcing children out of their beds at gunpoint and bulldozes their homes.

Salim rebuilt his home for the fourth time in 2003, again with the help of ICAHD. His family, too traumatized to live there, now rent a two-room house at the opposite edge of Anata. They have dedicated their former home, the very place we are sitting in, as a House of Peace, a place where local and international peace activists meet and where volunteers stay when they sign up to help ICAHD rebuild demolished homes. Salim's story is not just shocking and depressing, but inspirational. I am awed by his strength and non-violent reaction despite being violated over and over, a gentle soul with the unflappable patience of Job.

As a parent, I wonder what he tells his children, what he tells himself to move forward. How impossibly daunting it must be for Palestinian parents, their role of protector and provider compromised by Israeli authorities, knowing their children appreciate that they are powerless.

Is peace being stalled past the point of no return? What will that point look like? Do Israeli decision-makers hope the Palestinians will eventually give up and leave their land and homes?

"I received yet another demolition order against Beit Arabiya. They might come tomorrow or the day after," Salim continues. "My children are afraid to go from the bedroom to the bathroom at night, even though we don't live here anymore. We're going to take our case to the International Court. We want peace with justice. After the Oslo peace talks in 1993, the number of settlements doubled. There are 450,000 settlers in the West Bank now."

Sadly, Salim's story is not unique. As of July 4, 2009, ICAHD estimated that "24,145 houses have been demolished in the West Bank, East Jerusalem and Gaza since 1967." Another 20,000 to 40,000 homes are slated for demolition to make room for more walls and more exclusively Jewish colonies and by-pass roads on Palestinian lands.

As the group says goodbye to Salim, I notice he has replanted a variety of fruit trees in the yard. I pause to photograph a juvenile orange tree growing near the peace center. I am amazed to find it laden with oranges, thriving despite the arid environment, thriving for now despite the likelihood that one day Israeli bulldozers will arrive to knock it down.

"My father would love to see this orange tree," I tell Salim before departing. He immediately plucks a couple of oranges from one of its branches.

"Give these to your father," he says, handing me the oranges. "Tell him Salim sends his *salaams*."

I place them in the bottom of my backpack, intending to smuggle them back home to show my father, an avid gardener, who never stopped missing his family's fruit orchards in Kherbet Rouha, Lebanon, and who can still be found in his backyard early in the mornings, bent over, weeding or watering, pruning the grapevine or grafting a plum branch on an apple tree. He will be saddened, but not surprised, when I tell him Salim's story. He is aware of Israel's practice of demolishing Palestinian homes. Demolitions have become a normal part of life for Palestinians. But, like me, my father will be shocked to hear that Salim's house was demolished and rebuilt, not once, but four times, and he, too, will be inspired by Salim's perseverance and resilience. I can hear his response.

"God help him. God help them all."

And, in my mind's eye, I also see my father's blue eyes brighten when I hand him the two oranges from Palestine. He will not taste them right away. First, he'll marvel at their perfection and inhale their aroma, triggering memories of the *watan*, the homeland, back to being ten years old and stealing ripened fruit from the orchards at night. Eventually, he'll share the oranges with my mother and save the seeds. Later he'll plant the seeds indoors, knowing full well that even if they sprout and grow to become trees, they may not flourish or bear fruit. But that will not stop him from trying to grow an orange tree in Edmonton, Alberta, from Salim in occupied Palestine.

The story of Salim, Arabiya and their seven children, the destiny of Beit Arabiya Peace Center is still being written; it does not end here. In January of 2012, Israel demolished Beit Arabiya for the fifth time. The following summer, ICAHD volunteers rebuilt it, only for Israel to demolish it four months later in November of 2012, for the sixth consecutive time.

I discover on ICAHD's website that the group reconstructed Beit Arabiya in July of 2013, during which time I was in High River, Alberta, deployed by my department as an information officer, helping grieving flood victims, who had lost their homes and other belongings in a natural disaster, an "Act of God."

THREE

A *Moshav* Overlooking Gaza

There are demonstrations planned for January 1, 2012, in a number of places around the Gaza Strip. We will be there. The intent is to break the siege. Many Israelis have no knowledge of the siege. They don't want to know. They don't want to be reminded. There is complete indifference to it. Some Israelis yell at us. One Jewish man told us, 'Hitler didn't finish the job. He should have finished you too.'

Aliyah Strauss, Coalition of Women for Peace
October 20, 2009, Meeting at Colony Hotel, Jerusalem

By 7:00 AM on day three of our journey, the Arab-Jewish Women's Peace Coalition is on its way to southern Israel to visit a *moshav*, a farming cooperative, near Sderot, just one kilometre north of the Gaza Strip. After a two-hour drive, we arrive at a green oasis in the desert, named Netive Ha'asara. Its white homes with red-tiled roofs are spaced comfortably apart amid rolling sand dunes, sheltered by a diversity of trees: willow, cedar, palm, orange. And cactus pear and grape, and bougainvillea blooming in a variety of bright colours, contrast the pale terrain.

We are scheduled to meet Roni Keidar, a Jewish grandmother and peace activist with Other Voice, a group of Jewish residents of Sderot and the surrounding area, who advocate for a non-violent resolution to the "conflict" and work to reach out, using mobile phones to establish contact with Palestinians in Gaza.

Roni welcomes us with a warm smile and leads us to her spacious backyard, where we sit around a table, sipping juice, ready to hear her story. Her short grey hair frames a kind-looking face and she is wearing a bright, red t-shirt. She explains that her family used to live in a *moshav*, which Israel established in 1973 on the northern shore of the Sinai Peninsula.

"It was a fantastic success story. We knew it was occupied territory, but it didn't occur to us that one day we would be put out for peace, that we'd have to leave the settlement, ten years after it was built. It was a garden of paradise," she says wistfully.

"It was a choice: peace or land. The government selected this location; it's not far from the sea."

As part of a peace treaty with Egypt, Israel relocated the community to its current spot near Sderot, after withdrawing from the Sinai Peninsula, which it had captured from Egypt during the 1967 Arab-Israeli War. I am hoping Roni will also mention that Sderot sits overtop the ruins of Najd, formerly a Palestinian village, but she does not.

"I'm from England. I came to Israel as a little girl," she continues. "My husband is from Egypt. He came in 1967. We got married here, built our lives. We spent four years living in Cairo. My husband helped Egyptians enhance their agricultural techniques.

"I feel for the people in Gaza. But what could our government do? They have to protect us. Since the wall and closures, we have suffered from rockets, primitive ones, usually harmless, but no suicide bombers. We have an alert system and bomb shelters. There is a safe room in every house and there is a bomb shelter in the middle of the *moshav*. We have 20 seconds to get into one when there is a siren.

"Because of the Gaza closures, we are worried that at any time we will be hit with bombs and explosives. There must be mutual recognition. Our greenhouses were bombed three times."

As I listen, I think about how terrifying it must be for residents in the Sderot area. At the same time I think about the devastating impact of Israel's continued blockade of essential goods such as food, medical equipment and building materials into Gaza, and the mammoth concrete wall and buffer zone Israel built surrounding it, rendering the most densely populated areas in the world into what many have described as, "the largest prison on earth."

I am relieved to know that at least the people of Sderot have sirens and bomb shelters, but at the same time it hurts to know that the people of Gaza do not have such security measures. At least the people of Sderot are protected by one of the world's most sophisticated armies. The people living in the Gaza Strip have no army. Neither did they have protection from Israel's more recent 22-day war in the winter of 2008-2009, when its army killed of over 1,500 Palestinians. They had no place to hide from the 1,000-pound bombs that Israel dropped on them, with as little as a push of a button, from drones and fighter jets, no protection from laser-guided missiles Israel shot at them from war ships positioned off shore. The people of Gaza are trapped and literally have nowhere to hide. I want to say all this, but hold back, not wanting to be insensitive. I remind myself that it is futile to focus on which side is suffering more, as if it were some kind of competition.

"I felt sad for the innocent people of Gaza when Israeli planes were dropping bombs on them," Roni is saying.

The more she talks about Gaza the more I am reminded of my desire to see the place. I have read about the hell that is Gaza. I want to see it for myself, hear from Palestinians living there, but the *moshav* near Sderot is the closest I will get to seeing Gaza on this trip. Before our journey, our peace coalition decided it would be difficult and potentially dangerous to go there.

"I see the suffering on the other side," Roni says. "It's a tangled web. We need a vision. We need to build respect. As Jews, we should understand Palestinians, their identity and home. But understanding is not enough. We tried to exchange cards during Ramadan last year. We took sweets and went to the border. We had a permit, but Hamas said, 'No.'

"We do not know our enemy. We don't speak their language. They know ours. Our group is trying to create dialogue, but with whom? Rockets are used to eliminate Israel from the map, but they need to realize we are here. They are here. The siege of Gaza is the enemy. Leaders on both sides are busy investing in conflict, not holding hands."

We learn that her daughter's best friend was killed by a rocket fired from Gaza. Now, whenever she takes her grandchildren for walks, she is always thinking that she has only 20 seconds to run to the nearest shelter when the siren goes off.

—❧—

It is almost noon. I am back on the bus with our group to see the *moshav* and its surroundings. Roni sits at the front of the bus, directing the driver towards the center of the community.

"It's an underground shelter," she says, pointing to a non-descript structure.

I follow the path of her finger to where groups of children are playing outside a school, not far from the structure. I am curious to see what is inside, but I get only a glance at its entrance as we drive past. I would not have recognized it for what it was had Roni not pointed it out. The exterior of the square enclosure built around the entrance is made of concrete blocks more than a metre high and painted with brightly coloured murals: a pastoral landscape and smiling children. It is encircled by light posts painted a bright blue.

At the western outskirts of the *moshav*, we follow a single-lane paved road alongside a cement wall eight metres high. Gaza is to the west, hidden by the Wall. I notice the side of the Wall facing the *moshav* is painted the same colour as the orange sand in the surrounding area, presumably to hide its hideousness, to make it easier on the eye for residents. The bottom two-thirds of the Wall depicts a continuous rolling landscape of uniform sand dunes. A cement watchtower and steel communication tower rise well above the Wall, at least three times higher, dominating the skyline. When our bus veers away from the Wall, I look at it from a distance; it is barely distinguishable from the landscape. The painted, orange sand dunes on the Wall blend into the actual sand dunes it bisects, and the unpainted, upper, grey portion of the Wall and the sky above it appear as one expanse.

"Stop for us here so we can get out and walk around," Roni tells our driver.

He lets us out on a plateau that has a full view of the western horizon. I make my way to the far edge, staring out over the hillside. There is another segment of the Wall further down the slope. It is unpainted and seems to mark the edge of the military-imposed buffer, isolating the Gaza Strip from Israel. There is a military facility nearby. Soldiers in military jeeps drive along a road parallel to the Wall. I am mesmerized by the view, still disbelieving what I am witnessing.

And there it is.

Where the land meets the sky in the west, I catch sight of Gaza, only one kilometre away, walled in. The cluster of taller grey buildings appears ghost-like in the distance. I cannot see the piles of flattened homes and the gaping holes in schools and hospitals, left by the Israeli army earlier this year, but I know the ruins are there, behind the Wall. I cannot see the bewildered children, but I know they are there, playing amid piles of rubble, cement chunks and rebar where their homes once stood. I cannot see the displaced people living in tents or in crowded rooms with extended families, but I know they are there, homeless. I cannot see the survivors whose entire families were killed, but I know they are there, mourning. I cannot see the results of Israel's continued blockade of food and medicines into Gaza, but I know that thousands are there, hungry and hurting.

Noor, one of the Arab sisters in our coalition begins to cry when she sees the Wall isolating Gaza. I want to do the same. Or scream. Or throw stones. *But what good would that do?*

Noor has visited on numerous occasions and worked for a year in Ramallah. "The last time I was here," she says wiping her tears, "there were no walls."

We pose for photographs with the Wall and Gaza in the background. The truth hurts. At times it seems simpler not knowing the truth. I think about the Palestinians living there, literally under siege. I think, too, of Roni and the residents of the *moshav*; both communities, practically neighbours, living without genuine peace, in real fear of being injured or killed.

A short while later, we accompany Roni back to her home, where our driver drops her off and we part ways. As we head to our next destination, a meeting with a Bedouin women's organization for a demonstration on spinning wool, I imagine a different world if more women like Roni were in positions of power and had the audacity to try and affect change. At least here in this *moshav* one grandmother is trying to connect with the women in Gaza despite the obstacles.

—⁂—

A year and a half after our tour in Netive Ha'asara, members of Roni's group, The Other Voice, appeal in writing to Benjamin Netanyahu, the Prime Minister of Israel. Their April 30, 2010, letter posted on their website, www. othervoice.org, states in part:

> There is no justification for the continued siege that Israel has imposed on Gaza for a number of years. It will not bring us security. The opposite is true: the blockade is only harming Israel's safety because it deepens the hatred and the loathing, and it encourages acts of revenge and terror. This is a powder keg of desperation, frustration and fury that can explode at any moment. Ordinary citizens in Gaza are suffering from this blockade, while extremists are nourished and growing stronger by it every day.

In November of 2012, that part of the world becomes the powder keg Roni's group warned their Prime Minister about. Militant Palestinians launch rockets at Sderot. The Israeli army drops bombs on Gaza.

The Canadian Charger, an online weekly, publishes an article entitled, "Is Attacking Gaza Really about Hamas Rockets?" written by Stuart Littlewood on November 21, 2012. He quotes an untitled poem, whose author is unknown. For me, it sums up the situation in Gaza and elsewhere in the Occupied Palestinian Territories:

> They stole my land,
> burnt my olive trees,
> destroyed my house,
> took my water,
> bombed my country,
> imprisoned my father,
> killed my mother,
> took my job,
> starved us all,
> humiliated us all,
> But I am to blame: I shot a rocket back.
> So they stole more of my land,
> burnt my olive trees,
> destroyed my house, took my water,
> bombed my country....

FOUR

The Ghosts of Ein Hawd

Today I live with my family in Walaja village. It isn't really our village. We named it after our original village that we had to leave behind [in 1948, during the Nakba]. We can still see our village on the hillside across from us, but we aren't allowed to go there. My son Taha was taken to prison when he was thirteen. When he was in prison, he built a miniature replica of the Al Aqsa Mosque. He dreams of praying there one day, although the Israelis won't give Palestinian men a permit to pray there till they are over fifty. My son Mustafa is a farmer. This winter he was carrying firewood home to us. The Israeli soldiers stopped him and made him stand out in the rain till nightfall. They took his donkey and told him they were taking his donkey to prison.

Hind, poster on Israel's Separation Wall
Bethlehem, 2010

Palestinians want to tell their stories. I hear them everywhere I go, typical accounts that sound the same, tales of dispossession, displacement and oppression. Yet, there are also atypical stories begging to be heard.

Our bus travels west from the Oasis of Peace towards the villages of Ein Hawd and Ein Hod. Their names barely distinguishable in sound and spelling, both villages are located in the Caramel Mountains overlooking the Mediterranean Sea in northern Israel, about eight kilometres from the coastal city of Haifa. The morning is warm and I am already regretting the extra sweater I am wearing. I slip it off, wad it up and put it on the empty aisle seat beside me.

We are on our way to meet the descendants of one Palestinian family that Israel drove out of their village in 1948, along with 700 other villagers, and barred them from returning home. But, this one extended family remained close to their old village. Years later, they established a new village on a family-owned pasture two kilometres up the mountain and named it the New Ein Hawd. We are also going to visit the original 700-year-old Muslim village that Israel depopulated, turned it into a one-of-a-kind artist's colony and renamed it Ein Hod, one of a handful of Palestinian villages Israel did not destroy.

We are joined by Wafaa, an Israeli Arab, and Michal, an Israeli Jew; both women live and work at the Oasis of Peace. Leah, the matriarch of our peace coalition, asks if they will share their stories with us.

"Please tell us," Leah implores, in her song-like voice. "We'd love to hear them."

Wafaa, seemingly eager to tell her story, begins first. "My parents didn't raise us to hate Jews. That bothered me. Now I feel resentment. I have to be nice."

She sits near the front of the bus at the edge of her seat, facing us. She is tall and beautiful with wavy black hair and high cheekbones. She appears calm and composed, but I sense in her a dam of emotions aching to be freed. After glancing out the window, she continues.

"The year 1948 is still fresh. The people in my village fled to Lebanon. They walked there, without food. My mother was nine months pregnant. They took my dad and killed my paternal uncles. They were going to kill my father, too. But, he managed to escape and a month later joined my mother in a refugee camp in Lebanon."

Tears drown her eyes, tugging at my heart. I imagine my mother in Lebanon back in 1948, separated from my father, who left earlier that same year for Brazil out of economic necessity. Twenty years old at the time, with barely enough food for her and my two sisters, my mother shared what food she had with Palestinian refugees who ended up in her tiny mountain village.

"I was born in 1961," Wafaa tells us. "My father was especially quiet as we were growing up. He used to work as a policeman. He lost his job and had to start from scratch. Still, my parents didn't say the Jews are our enemy.

"I moved to Neve Shalom-Wahat al-Salaam after I got married. We feel as equals there and appreciated as people."

She pauses for a breath.

"But, there is no one to teach Palestinian history. The history of my father is not taught. I grew up here and learned Jewish history, but not Palestinian, only bits and pieces. How is that fair?" her eyebrows rise in emphasis. "How can we justify each other's existence? We proposed to build a small museum to tell the stories of the *Nakba,* but the idea was rejected at Neve Shalom."

I listen as she tries squeezing decades of displacement into a 10-minute monologue. It is clear Wafaa is grateful she ended up at the Oasis of Peace; most Palestinians are not as fortunate. Still, I detect the illusion of equality is just that, an illusion, combined with issues of identity, loss of connection to the land and culture and a deep yearning for the *watan,* the "homeland." I never fully appreciated my own father's longing and emotional attachment for Lebanon. Even though he has already purchased his burial plot in a tiny Muslim cemetery on the outskirts of Edmonton, he still says in a melancholy voice, "I wish I could die in the *watan.*" Poverty forced him to leave his beloved homeland, but he never stopped adoring it and feeling connected to it on some profound level.

Yet, for my mother, the *watan* is a different story. She has no desire to return to her homeland. More often than not, she says, "God build Canada." Ordinary things will trigger this daily invocation: like when her neighbour, a German couple, shovels her sidewalks after a heavy snowfall, or when the garbage collectors make their weekly rounds, or when the dentist fixes her aching tooth. I have never once heard her invoke the same prayer for Lebanon.

I remember vividly my mother's reaction the day she returned home to Edmonton following her first and only visit back to Lebanon after almost thirty years. The faces of her neighbours looking on in curiosity, no sooner did she step out of the car in front of her house and she is on her knees kissing the ground. She never got over the hardships she endured as a young mother in the *watan* after my father left for Brazil. Penniless, my mother was compelled to scour the mountainside at night in search of firewood and haul her stash home in bundles on her back like a mule, and to labour all day in the family fields, hunger gnashing her insides as she hand-harvested the small plot of wheat she grew to feed her family. Once, she chased after a village cat that stole her piece of meat, a rarity to eat. My mother retrieved her meat, washed it off and made it into *kibee*. Six years had lapsed in this way before she and my sisters were able to join my father in Brazil.

For me, my *watan* is Canada, not Brazil, where I was born, not Lebanon where I trace my ancestry. It was not until I visited Lebanon for the first time in 1978 that I began to appreciate better that amorphous connection for myself. That feeling became more acute when Israel invaded Lebanon in 1982 and killed a family member living in the Bekaa Valley.

I assume Wafaa feels safe now and happy to be living at the Oasis of Peace, but it is not home. Her family made it back to Palestine, now Israel, but not to her ancestral village. It was destroyed, planted over with trees and literally erased from the map, but I sense it will remain in her memory, a fire that cannot be extinguished.

"There are no museums in Israel to illustrate Palestinian history," she says after a brief moment. "No monuments placed where Palestinians were killed. No one to tell the untold stories. We were blocked. When all the survivors of the *Nakba* die, what will happen?

"I studied in a Christian school. I learned about others' history. What about *my* history?" she asks in a pained voice.

We are all silent. I think about what it means to be denied your own story.

"In 1978, I wrote about my history for a school assignment," she continues. "The Minister of Education himself came to my school to say, 'No, No' — to a 16-year-old girl! I wasn't even allowed to tell my story. I was marked as a troublemaker.

"We need a museum to tell the Palestinian stories. Israel's expulsion ideology of a maximum land and minimum people is not told."

Wafaa tells us she sent one of her daughters to study in Victoria, British Columbia, where she hopes her daughter will gain more confidence about her identity.

"There, she can tell her story without being pushed away," Wafaa says. "It's a big sacrifice. My other daughter is 13 years old. She constantly wants to hang Palestinian icons on her bedroom walls. She also wants to carry a Palestinian symbol. But there's fear. It takes its toll, to explain, to keep saying 'No.'"

Our driver follows a highway north through Israel's coastal plain. We pass banana plantations, grape orchards and wineries while Michal recounts the history of the villages of Ein Hod and Ein Hawd. I am surprised to learn she has a personal connection to the original Palestinian village of Ein Hawd. Her dark hair is pinned back, accentuating big brown eyes. She is sitting across the aisle from Wafaa, wearing a pink, knee-length Bohemian-style shirt and white pants.

"Ein Hawd is frozen in time," Michal tells us. "About 40 people, belonging mainly to one extended family, refused to leave and hid in the caves further up the slope from their former village.

"Most villages were destroyed after they were depopulated. The villagers of Ein Hawd would watch from above as Jewish immigrants moved in. It was an open wound. They lived it every day. Bitterness.

"My mother was 14 when her parents moved to Israel in 1949. Her family was put on a train to a camp and later taken to live in Ein Hawd. My mother told me, 'The houses had everything, clothes, cutlery, furniture, pantries filled with food. They were left, as if their owners were simply away for a holiday.'"

Soon after the Jewish immigrants moved in, they began claiming the houses were haunted; they were spooked and abandoned them. The village stayed empty for more than a year. I have not decided yet if I believe in ghosts, but I would be spooked, too, and imagine the ghosts of those who were forced to flee, crouching in the corners of their homes at night, scaring people, refusing to leave, yelling, "This is *my* home."

"It's a unique situation," Michal continues. "The old people of Ein Hawd would walk around staring at their homes, and at the mosque, which had been converted into a restaurant and bar, a place known for having the wildest parties. They can see their homes, but they cannot touch them."

A group of artists from Europe belonging to the Dada movement transformed the old village into an artists' colony in 1953. They decided to preserve it, keep the place as is. I do not know much about the Dada movement, but I do know it is fundamentally an anti-war art movement that began in Zurich, Switzerland, in response to World War I. A voice within nags me. Isn't the dispossession of the indigenous people of Ein Hawd contrary to the Dada movement? How can the creators of the artists' colony, members of an anti-war movement, reconcile the fact the 700-year-old village was taken in an act tantamount to war? Is the history of this ancient village passed on to the many tourists who flock to it each year? Are its current residents aware of the village's history? How can they not know?

I marvel at the passing landscape as our driver takes us through forested hills of tamarisk, cypress, pine, carob and oak. And interspersed are towering eucalyptus trees. Non-natives.

For decades, the Jewish National Fund has been planting millions of eucalyptus trees, indigenous only to Australia, presumably because the aromatic tree is beneficial, fast growing, adaptable and drought resistant. I know from working with foresters that eucalyptus is also highly flammable and needs fire to propagate. After many years of planting, it has become ubiquitous on the land in Israel.

Tenacious eucalyptus roots stretch deep into the earth in search of water, out of sight, while their graceful canopies have become a curtain, concealing former Palestinian villages: razed homes, schools, cemeteries and mosques, hiding what happened. But, not all things can be covered up.

We wind our way up the slope through pines and olive groves to the New Ein Hawd, where today about 300 people live. We arrive at a green, two-story, U-shaped building with a large yellow sign attached to an iron fence out front. In Arabic and Hebrew it says, *Albeet fe Ein Hawd*, which translates into "House in Ein Hawd." It is an Arabic restaurant and also functions as an information center and residence. It is owned and operated by Mohamed al-Hija and his extended family.

We climb a set of stairs to the second floor, where we are greeted by Mohamed's petite teenage daughter. The open space has a cozy living room to one side and a bright restaurant area lined with large picture windows. I gaze out at the view down the mountain from the New Ein Hawd. It is breathtaking. The original village further down the slope is camouflaged by lush vegetation. In the distance, the Mediterranean Sea shimmers bluer than the sky. Nothing seems amiss. I snap a few photographs, wondering how the villagers coped. How can they put the past behind them and move on when that past persists in constant view?

Would have it been easier on them if their original village had been destroyed?

I take a seat on one of the sofas, as do the rest of the women, in front of a television. Mohamed's daughter inserts a DVD into the player and sits down. We watch a documentary entitled, *Not On Any Map*, detailing the history of the New Ein Hawd, once an "unrecognized village" (meaning the village did not have access to any services: no water, no electricity, no roads, no medical clinics, hospitals or schools). The film features Mohamed, who founded the Association of Forty and petitioned Israel for official recognition of the New Ein Hawd, which was eventually granted in 1992, though Israel did not provide it with water and electricity infrastructure until 2005.

A moment near the end of the documentary, when the new village is finally granted access to water, is especially poignant. Mohamed and members of his family are filmed as they take a jug of water to the cemetery and pour it over his father's grave, the patriarch of the large extended family who helped establish the new village. They endured and finished what he had started. The family's tribute, the happy ending, warms my heart. Knowing me, tonight I will release all the pent-up emotions I manage to stifle and cry in the darkness, unseen, after my roommate falls asleep and her steady breathing fills the silence.

After watching the documentary, I get to meet Mohamed, who is a civil engineer. I walk over to the office area. He is standing behind the counter, smoking a cigarette and talking with some of the women. He has a rosy complexion and his hair is cropped short. His sparkling blue eyes, the same shade of blue as the shirt he is wearing, stand out.

"We were deemed squatters on our own land," he says tiredly, taking a drag of his cigarette. A ring of smoke emerges, hovers above his head and disappears.

"We were told, 'You left. You can't come back. You exist, but you don't exist.'

"The children would ask, 'Why do the cows and goats have water and we don't?'"

He props his elbow on the counter, pausing, as if to allow his words to penetrate.

"But if you sleep you get nothing," he smiles. "The New Ein Hawd is now recognized by Israel. Now it's on the map."

"What does it mean to be a Palestinian?" Mohamed asks at one point, as if he is ruminating out loud. "Where do we belong? I do not believe in any flag. I just want to live in peace. Under any flag. Under any government. I just want my village. I didn't move from Palestine."

His every word fills me with admiration and intrigue. Mohamed has no desire to reclaim his former village or to move back into his ancestral home. He wants simply to live in peace in the New Ein Hawd. He is the first Palestinian I have met who admitted he cares less about which flag flies over his country. This surprises me the most. The rooftops in his former village below are a relentless reminder of the past, yet it seems he has somehow managed to reconcile and rise above the past. Numerous questions flit through my mind. I want to understand the lesson here, have a one-on-one conversation with him. I open my mouth to speak, a question on the tip of my tongue. But I hesitate a second too long. Noor begins to stir, checking her watch, a sign that it is time to go.

Our driver heads a couple kilometres further down the mountain to the old Ein Hawd, now a Jewish artist's colony, renamed Ein Hod, a Hebrew variation of the original name meaning "Spring of Glory." It is common practice for Israeli officials to assign new names to former Palestinian landmarks and villages. It is one way of claiming ownership and erasing the past. Ironically, many Hebrew words are the same in Arabic so the Palestinian presence and past are not as easily erased. For instance, the word *Ein*, which forms part of both names, means "spring" in both languages, and was chosen because a natural spring likely exists in the area. I am always fascinated by the story behind the name of a person or place.

The mini-bus weaves through a section of the ancient village. It is an artist's paradise where the natural splendour, cornucopia of colours, abundant sun and salty breath of the sea unleash one's creativity and allow it to bloom. I am struck by the original, rustic stone houses, still standing, silent testaments to the souls who once lived here. Converted into art studios, workshops, galleries and museums, including accommodations for tourists, these houses peer through a veil of pink, yellow and orange bougainvillea. Honeysuckle and morning glory crawl along stone fences. Bunches of iris and birds of paradise line cobbled walkways. The place appears idyllic, its dark history invisible. The utopian facade seems to taunt me as we drive past without stopping.

The ancient depopulated Palestinian village of Ein Hawd, the once-upon-a-time-before-1948 Ein Hawd, whose name in Arabic translates into, "Spring of the Trough," and whose former residents trace their genealogy back to one of Saladin's generals who won the territory from the Crusaders, remains—but only as a phantom.

I have no way of knowing as we drive away that a year from now, on December 2, 2010, the two villages of Ein Hod and New Ein Hawd and the forested slopes of olive, pine and eucalyptus will make the news around the world when they are threatened by wildfire. Residents will be evacuated. The two villages will join forces to help each other. Israel, the military might, will be ill-prepared to fight the wildfire. The Palestinian Authority and the international community will offer firefighting resources. I will feel pride when the Alberta government, my department, guardians of Alberta's forests and forest communities, offers two CL215 fire bombers along with an air attack officer, who happens to be a co-worker. However, these firefighting resources will not require deployment. The wildfire, reportedly the worst in Israel's history, will be extinguished, but not before the 43 deaths of volunteer firefighters, including a teenager, and police officers, and not before damaging or destroying some of the original homes in Ein Hod and parts of the adjacent forested slopes.

The New Ein Hawd will be saved. Fire does not distinguish; it destroys in order to renew, a natural and necessary phenomenon.

As we continue north to Haifa, Michal breaks the silence in the bus. "There's no recognition or admission," she says. "There's a movement now to re-tell stories. The horrors are not told, and there are other villages. More than 400 villages can't be visited. It's kind of creepy."

My mind wanders back to the ghosts of Ein Hawd, who frightened away the first occupiers, only for the village to be rescued by an anti-war art movement and transformed into an artist's colony. Even a writer cannot make up such stories. I feel like crying and laughing at the same time.

Have the ghosts given up? Or do they still linger in Ein Hawd? Perhaps they are trapped inside a clay statue or entombed in a piece of amber fashioned into a pendant or quieted under the layers of paint on an artist's canvas.

FIVE

Breaking the Silence: The "Sterilization" of the Heart of Hebron

It takes time to realize that for three years we were not human beings. We were some sort of Zombies, not making our own decisions, carrying things out without a second's thought. If they'd tell me, and they did tell me, to shut some old lady up by sticking the gun's handle into her stomach—I'd do it without even thinking.

First Sergeant, Yael – elite unit
Breaking the Silence Testimonial, Booklet #1, 2005-2007

We pay 50 shekels each (about $15 Canadian) and board an air-conditioned bus on Ben Yehuda Street across from Jerusalem Central Bus Station. I take a window seat and fish inside my camera bag for a pen and notepad. A middle-aged man wearing a black *kippa* sits next to me without looking or speaking.

We are heading out on a non-traditional tour of the heart of Hebron, now a "sterilized zone," an area where Israel has largely "cleansed" the indigenous Palestinian population from as if they were germs or noxious weeds. Hebron is the second largest city in the Occupied Palestinian Territories, an ancient, continuously-inhabited city, a holy place for Jews, Christians and Muslims. But, for Palestinians still living in its city center, Hebron is a hellish place.

The nine members of our peace coalition are joined by two Palestinian women from the Oasis of Peace, where we are staying. About 20 others, local Israelis and internationals, are also on board.

Our guide, Yehuda Shaul, stands at the front of the bus facing us, sporting a crisp, white dress shirt, cargo shorts and safari hat. He is tall and stocky with a dark, thick beard and moustache. From the moment I set eyes on him, I sense he will leave an indelible imprint on me.

"I'm an observant orthodox Jew," he begins, as our bus leaves West Jerusalem. "I was a combat soldier in the Israeli army for about three years, served in Hebron for 14 months, and later became a commander. Towards the end of my service, in March 2004, I began thinking about my life as a civilian. For the first time I asked myself, 'Who is Yehuda? It was an obscene reality. I didn't want to believe I did all those terrible things. I felt something went wrong. I couldn't continue my life without doing something. But what? I started talking to some of my comrades and discovered we all felt the same. We could no longer stay quiet. That's how the idea for Breaking the Silence started."

I learned of Breaking the Silence during the coalition's planning meetings. It is a group comprised of 700 Israeli combatants and ex-combatants between 20 and 29 years old. They gather testimonies about soldier experiences and publish them in newspapers, booklets and on the Internet. The group also gives about 300 lectures a year, targeting Israeli youth. They began by having a photo exhibition about Hebron in Tel Aviv. Over 7,000 people attended. Some of the people who attended were soldiers recently discharged from the army.

"Something remarkable happened during the exhibition," Yehuda says. "Many walked up to us saying, 'This picture you have on the wall, I have the same one from Gaza.' We realized our story was not unique."

His words captivate me. I notice I have been holding my breath, and immediately think of my son and daughters back home. I can't wait to tell them, and others, about Yehuda Shaul. Until now, I had not given much thought to the impact of Israel's military occupation on the occupier, its soldiers, and for the first time I contemplate the emotional and mental cost on the many men and women, who do not make the rules, but serve to enforce them and maintain the status quo. And while I have read about Israelis who refuse to serve in the military, Refuseniks, I never imagined I would one day meet an Israeli soldier, let alone one who feels remorse for his actions, or that I would see the power of redemption first-hand. I never thought I would feel sympathy towards the soldiers who enforce the Occupation. I know it is silly, but I feel compelled to hug Yehuda and tell him he is going to be alright, that the God of everyone and everything is most merciful and most forgiving.

"Breaking the Silence is not here to solve the Israeli-Palestinian conflict," Yehuda clarifies. "Our role is simple. We want to force society to look in the mirror at the reality. To listen to what we are doing, to question our moral boundaries. What is acceptable? What is not? The goal of Breaking the Silence is not just to tell horror stories about life for Palestinians in the West Bank and Gaza. Our goal is to help people understand the mindset of the Occupation — to understand the mindset of the occupier."

The bus travels south on Highway 60. The sun is a white disk, the cloudless sky a cerulean blue. We pass reddish slopes dotted with olive trees. Their distinctive silvery-green leaves and stout, gnarled trunks are so much a part of this land, embedded in the cultural and historical narratives of both Arab and Jew. We traverse verdant valleys, rolling stone terraces of grape and fig. Patches of carob and almond. Pomegranate and pistachio. I marvel at the bountiful hills.

I notice, too, that many of the highest hilltops have been seized for Israeli "outposts" and "settlements." Even out here, amid the natural spectacle, I cannot escape the Occupation. About 10 kilometres south of Jerusalem, Beit Jala, an ancient Palestinian Christian village, sits on a hilltop. Gilo, a Jewish settlement, which has been annexed to the municipality of Jerusalem, is perched on a higher hill. The United Nations deemed Gilo (and other settlements) illegal because they are built on the Palestinian side of the Green Line, the boundary between Israel and Palestine set out by the British Mandate in 1948. Across from Gilo, hidden by massive, concrete walls, is Bethlehem. We cross a bridge over a deep gorge separating Beit Jala from Gilo, part of the Tunnels Highway, built exclusively for Israeli use. We traverse a checkpoint and a tunnel under Gilo, and pass more Palestinian villages, some completely encircled by concrete walls eight metres high.

We continue along Highway 60, which closely follows an ancient road through a mountain chain, stretching from Jenin in the north to Be'er Sheva in the south. This access route has been used continuously for millennia. I romanticize how my Levantine ancestors, including the region's numerous conquerors and liberators, would have used this travel corridor.

I have a profound affinity for this land, but feel melancholic knowing I am witnessing a vanishing vista. The continued colonization of Palestine is clearly visible on the land. Every new settlement, every kilometre of exclusively Jewish road and every section of the Wall not only diminishes the natural flora and fauna, but also reduces the chance for peace and a viable Palestinian state. It is like the land is being eaten alive. Paradoxically, Israel is a leader in irrigation technology and has turned certain parts of the West Bank into oases. I saw this for myself when our group toured a *moshav*, an agricultural cooperative, near Sedrot, a desert region. But at the same time, this land is also being systematically destroyed in the name of security and to fulfill expansionist dreams of building a Greater Israel. Here, good fences do not make good neighbours I muse, not when those fences are cement monsters over three stories tall. Not when those fences serve as prison walls. Not when those fences turn Palestinian villages into ghettos.

"Hebron is different. It's not a national or political issue," Yehuda explains as we near the city. "It's a religious story for both sides. King David started here, ruling in the 15th century after the Jews were expelled from Spain. They settled in Hebron, integrating with the local Arab Muslim culture and speaking Arabic. In the 18th century, another wave of Jews from Europe, Ashkenazi Jews, became part of the city.

"On August 29, 1929, there was a brutal massacre against the Jewish community in Hebron. Sixty-seven were murdered, over 100 more were wounded, women were raped, property destroyed. But over 300 Jews were saved by their Palestinian neighbours. And, we all know what happened in 1948. Jordan occupied Hebron. In 1967, Israel conquered, liberated, or occupied, whichever terminology you prefer, the West Bank. Every Israeli government since has surrendered to settler demands. In the 1970s, the question was what to do with the occupied lands. Hebron is in the center of the south part of the West Bank. They divided Hebron in half, an east side and a west side, H1 and H2."

H1 represents 80 percent of Hebron and falls under the jurisdiction of the Palestinian Authority. H2 comprises 20 percent of Hebron: the city center, its commercial and industrial zones, an area connecting the north and south sides of the city and contains many sacred historical landmarks. The Israeli army controls this area.

At the outskirts of the city, our bus stops on the side of the road. Yehuda pulls out his mobile phone and dials.

"We have to wait here for a bit for our police escort," he tells us after finishing his call.

My stomach churns at the thought of needing a police escort, the uncertainty of what might happen. Surely, our large group is going to draw unwanted attention.

Will the police escort make our passage safe? Whose side will they be on?

Yehuda continues.

"Hebron is the most violent place in the West Bank. There are 160,000 Palestinians and 800 settlers. There are over 2,000 soldiers and hundreds of Israeli police, yet there is no law enforcement. Israeli civil law doesn't apply because Hebron is under military control. Soldiers receive orders to protect the settlers, many of whom are armed, but not the Palestinians. Hebron is a laboratory. It is about making our presence felt: eight-hour shifts, police patrols, raiding homes at night, shooting bullets, lighting fires. Between 2001 and 2003, we enforced 377 days of full curfews and 500 days of partial curfews. The unemployment rate for Palestinians rose to 80 percent. It's the worst humanitarian situation in the West Bank."

He walks down the aisle, passing out a brochure produced by B'Tselem, the Israeli Information Center for Human Rights in the Occupied Palestinian Territories and the Association for Civil Rights in Israel. I take one from him and unfold it on my lap. One side is a colour-coded map showing the location of Israeli settlements embedded in the city: Tel Rumeida, Beit

Romano, Avraham Avinu and others. The map also shows the various types of restrictions on Palestinian movement through the heart of the city, a "security zone." I stare in disbelief at the different-coloured streets, labelled "completely closed," streets where "travel is forbidden," streets where both "shops have been closed and travel is forbidden." It breaks my heart. Thousands of years of human habitation and evolution have come down to this, a piece of paper indicating the streets where its Palestinian denizens cannot even set foot.

Yehuda holds up the map, pointing our route and explains that more than 1,000 Palestinian families fled from the area we will be visiting. Israel's military occupation, its confiscation of Palestinian shops and homes, together with settler violence, closed streets and military curfews, have rendered Hebron's city center into a "ghost town." I study the map further, appreciating the bird's eye view of our destination.

Segregation at work.

Ten minutes later, our bus is following two police jeeps.

"Please stick together," Yehuda warns. "Stay close to the police and ignore any settler who might yell at you."

"Can we take photographs?" I ask above the din of stirrings, paper crinkling and the muffled conversations of passengers.

"That would be fine," he replies. "Just don't aim your camera on the soldiers."

I cannot help wondering what would happen if I inadvertently, or advertently, snapped a photograph of a soldier.

How much leniency is there for tourists and peace activists?

The bus stops on a sloping street and we disembark. Two squads of Israeli riot police surround us, for protection from the settlers. There are Israeli soldiers everywhere I look: atop roofs, walking about, sitting in jeeps, standing in watchtowers and sniper towers, manning checkpoints. I stick close to one of the women in our coalition. The presence of violence is everywhere. It is unnerving. I fear for my life.

We walk up a steep road leading to the Tel Rumeida and Admot Yishai settlements, higher up on top of a hill and completely embedded in the Palestinian neighbourhood. This road is "completely closed" to Palestinians, even those who live along it. When I glance back, Noor is steadying Leah, who is having difficulty walking up the sloped road, so Noor is staying back with her. On either side of them, two policemen remain to stand watch.

At the top of the hill, we take another road to the left and make our way across a walkway to a two-story, box-shaped house. It is the home of Issa Omro, a 29-year-old Palestinian, an electrical engineer and peace activist in Hebron. Stairs lead to the top level, a square outdoor terrace with a roof. Its open sides are protected by metal mesh. The group crowds in. I am glad to find an empty spot on the floor along a wall and squeeze in between two people.

Issa, the Arabic name for Jesus, waits near the top of the stairs for everyone to settle in. He is a slimmer version of Yehuda; they could pass for brothers.

"Settlers throw stones. Then they tell the army it was the Palestinians who attacked," he begins. "I document settler attacks on video and file complaints with the police, but it doesn't do any good. Once, I slept outside the police station, waiting to complain, only to be told, 'It's okay.'

"There are two different laws. It is apartheid."

I take notes, as do many in the group. Others audio or videotape him. I hear the frustration and pain in his voice. I am aware of the quietness in the open room when he pauses, the scratching sound of my pen against the page.

"A month ago, two Palestinians were walking in the hills," he tells us. "Three settlers attacked them. I was there and filmed the assault. The police arrested them, but later that day the two were set free. And they will do more. There's no punishment for their crimes. We have some crazy fanatics. The soldiers actually help the settlers.

"Last week, some settlers blocked a road. An ambulance carrying a sick elderly woman tried to get through the barrier. They broke the ambulance windows. One of them followed the ambulance, beating on it while the head of the army watched. He didn't care. We don't feel safe. Some settlers have even attacked the police. I filmed one beating and gave the tape to the investigator. Later, I was told that no report had been filed. And, I find out, the policeman who had been beaten didn't even report the incident. He knows the settler is stronger than him.

"If I throw a stone, as a Palestinian I would be jailed for six months. But, if a settler does the same, or worse, he just gets fined."

Issa stops and takes a sip from his water bottle.

"Yesterday, I was called when some Palestinian kids wanted to cross a checkpoint. Four soldiers kicked and beat them for ten minutes, for nothing. No one believes, but I have the beating on video. There is no law in the army. The soldiers tell me, 'I am the law, donkey.'"

The word "donkey" hits a visceral nerve, as if directed at me. Yehuda whispers something into Issa's ear. I assume he wants him to wrap it up. Issa asks if anyone needs to use the bathroom, explaining that the walking part of the tour will take hours and where we are heading, there are no bathrooms. A teenage boy appears and leads several people at a time down the outside stairs to a bathroom somewhere. Issa continues for those of us who remain.

"The main street in Hebron has been closed for six years. The settlers stole all the shops, the gold market. They set fires using Palestinian furniture for fuel. I'm afraid. They will kill. The settlers are armed with M16s. I'm more scared of the settlers than the army."

"Why do the Palestinians remain, living under such conditions?" a woman sitting next to me asks.

I'm curious too. Her question brings to mind interviews I saw with people in the southern United States, who were asked why they stayed in those areas despite the racism they faced daily. Each one answered the same way.

"Because this is my home," they would say. "This is where my family has lived for hundreds of years."

Without hesitating, Issa answers, "Their history, family and life are here. They are willing to suffer. It's considered shameful to leave. Neighbours who stay will think you're a collaborator."

We leave Issa's house, following Yehuda. It's sweltering even though it's still mid-morning. I wipe the beads of sweat from my forehead. As we cross a stone walkway through Issa's yard, a young Jewish man in the adjacent settlement, who looks more like an Arab than I do, jeers at us.

"You like Arab?" he laughs.

I ignore him. As an Arab, I do not find the rhetorical question particularly amusing. It hurts, adds to my growing fear, and I am somewhat thankful my *Arabness* does not show.

We are flanked on all sides by Israeli police as the group makes its way back down the steep road to Shuhada Street, where the bus dropped us off. Noor and Leah rejoin the group. Surprisingly, many in the group take photographs, even photographs of the police and the soldiers. I am fearful to do the same and feel conspicuous with my professional SLR. Then I notice a white-haired lady with a Nikon camera and a long telephoto lens who seems to have no fear photographing squads of soldiers. Encouraged by this, I lag near the back of the group so I can photograph the street where we just walked, sneaking some shots of the navy blue police jeep in the middle of the road as it inches behind us, and of the police squadron encircling us.

We come to a checkpoint 20 metres away that blocks Shuhada Street from the north. The beige trailer-like structure takes up the entire width of the road, sandwiched by three-story, stone buildings. It has two narrow passageways for north and south-bound pedestrian traffic only. I aim my camera at the checkpoint, focusing on the two soldiers standing sentry, checking a Palestinian woman's ID. They are boyish looking, like so many soldiers that I have observed so far. One looks right at me through the viewfinder as I release the shutter. I feel the blood rush to my face and quickly duck into the middle of the group, not daring to look back.

We turn right and head south on Shuhada Street. I contemplate the two meanings of "shuhada" in Arabic. One is witness. The other is martyr. Perhaps my mind is searching for meaning where there is none. I wonder how this street got its name. Here I am—witnessing what has become of Witness Street or Martyr Street. Witnessing Jewish settlers' taking of the commercial heart of Hebron, a place where the oppressor continues oppressing and making martyrs. I feel by witnessing this place, I, too, have become a martyr.

Shuhada Street is eerily quiet. Yehuda leads without speaking, allowing us to experience the silence for ourselves. The reports I read to prepare for this journey were not embellishments or lies: Hebron's city center *is* a ghost town. I feel as if I am walking through the deserted set of a Hollywood western. I half expect to see tumbleweeds roll across the street.

We walk through a block-long section, lined on both sides by two-story buildings made of Jerusalem stone, yellowed and damaged by the elements and neglect. Strings of electrical wires crisscross the walls like a spider's web. Most of the apartments on the top level are empty. Ground-level shops and businesses have been sealed up and abandoned. Cyan-coloured metal awnings above the entrances and doorways stand out. Dappled with rust. Dusty. Reminders of better times where gold shops, banks and other businesses once flourished. Their matching cyan-coloured doors are covered with black Stars of David and graffiti in Hebrew:

DEATH TO ARABS.

It reminds me of the marking of Jewish homes and businesses by the Nazis. It is the same hate, a uniquely human trait repeating itself. The only differences are who the *other* is and the geographic location.

Surprisingly, a few Palestinian families still live here, held hostage by settlers, languishing behind barred-up windows and balconies, cages they built to protect them from stones, garbage and other debris thrown by settlers. The front doors of these homes are located on this street, but banned from use. Yehuda stops to explain that to enter their homes, these Palestinians are forced to climb stairs or ladders onto neighbouring roofs to access other doors or back windows. I am curious to know what would happen in a medical emergency or fire.

Yehuda earlier referred to Shuhada Street as a "sterile zone." I consider his choice of words. Something or someone who is sterile is either free from unwanted germs or unable to produce offspring. It occurs to me that both definitions are apt. Israel succeeded in sterilizing Shuhada Street from the unwanted Palestinians and decimating the chance of freedom and economic growth, threatening their very survival.

Shuhada Street is a living cliché; it does defy words. I imagine stumbling over my words as I describe it to my co-workers when I am back home. Experiencing this place does not require the suspension of disbelief like watching a Hollywood film production. Rather, I find myself feeling the suspension of belief as I witness this place.

Where are you, Mr. Spielberg? Where are you, Oprah? Have you heard about Hebron?

I make a vow to myself and promise the ghosts of those who were driven out, and those who remain living as ghosts, to tell as many people as I can, and like Yehuda, do my part to "break the silence" about the cycle of violence in Hebron. I do not know how or when, but know I must try.

My fears suddenly dissipate. Heaviness lifts from my shoulders as I point my camera at everything I can see, documenting what a sterilized street looks like. With each click of the shutter, I capture a thousand words worth to help explain the unbelievable, the take-over of the commercial heart of Hebron by armed, Jewish immigrants with the help of the Israeli army. Imagine, for instance, Toronto's Yonge Street or Edmonton's Jasper Avenue being depopulated and seized from its rightful owners by foreigners.

I point my camera up at a narrow balcony on the second floor of a building. There is a little girl, no more than five years old, with her arms wrapped protectively around her younger brother from behind. Two little birds in a cage. She looks down at me with large, brown eyes, eyes wizened before their time. She is unafraid and smiles faintly. I smile back even though I feel like weeping. I imagine she has had to learn quickly to distinguish between settlers, soldiers, and tour groups led by Yehuda. The street in front of her home is a classroom where violence and racism are part of the daily lesson. I take a photograph and catch up to the group, contemplating their lost innocence and what will likely become of them.

We pass Beit Hadassah; a navy blue sign in front tells visitors its story. It was built by Hebronite Jews in 1893, and provided medical care to both Jews and Arabs. In 1967, a group of women and their children regained Jewish control over the building by squatting in it. No one stopped them and they have continued to live on site, expanding to a new settlement in the Palestinian neighbourhood east of Shuhada Street.

Shuhada Street curves to the west, where we stop in the shade of a tree across four one-story buildings. Their exterior walls are painted with colourful murals depicting the Jewish history in Hebron. Above each mural are white signs placed against a violet-coloured wall, each with a written account in English and Hebrew. The signs read:

ROOTS OF THE JEWISH PEOPLE, A PIOUS COMMUNITY,
DESTRUCTION AND LIBERATION, RETURN, REBUILDING.

We come to a long, sloping block, similar to the one we saw earlier. Rows of two-story buildings line the east and west sides of the street; most are abandoned shops and homes. They have the same rusting, cyan-coloured awnings and doors. Windows on the top floor and balconies are protected by burgundy cages. Even the weeds here are territorial, different types, now dry clumps, poke through cracks in the stone and cement walls, claiming their divinely-ordained piece of this place. All the streets intersecting Shuhada Street that we pass are blocked by cement barriers. It is staggering to witness. Here, too, a few Palestinian families remain, virtual prisoners. A boy peeks from behind a blanket draped over one of the balconies. He waves at me. I wave back. We do this several times. I wish I could remove his shackles.

We stop across from what used to be Hebron's outdoor market. Another Israeli settlement spills down the hillside east of the old market. A young Jewish boy, wearing a multi-coloured kippa, pedals past us on his bicycle without looking, unafraid and free to move about and play. Yehuda holds up photographs of the market before the street was "sterilized" in 2002, bursting with prosperous and happy shoppers and sellers, rows of tables stacked high with fruit and vegetables. The site is now marked by a white sign with red lettering, which reads:

THE ARABS STOLE THIS LAND FOLLOWING THE MURDER
OF 67 HEBRON JEWS IN 1929.

Behind us to the west is another blocked road, bisecting a Muslim cemetery. A three-story watchtower made of white Jerusalem stone looms in the middle of the road; parked beside it is an army jeep with soldiers sitting inside. There is another army jeep and four more soldiers blocking the south end of Shuhada Street, only a few metres from where our group is standing. One of the soldiers is a young woman who looks barely 18. Yehuda explains the site was purchased by a rabbi, who cannot sell it and now rents it to the settlers.

As Yehuda talks, I look back and notice we are being watched by two women, orthodox Jews dressed in traditional black dresses. They stand about 20 metres away on the opposite side of the street. Both of them have their arms crossed, presenting an imposing tableau. It is clear we are not welcome. A few minutes later, a school bus stops next to them. A group of children emerges. They see us and begin to yell in unison, sounding as if their words have been rehearsed. I do not understand what they are saying in Hebrew. But some words do not need a translation, the glares and looks of disdain say it all. It is frightening, dehumanizing, and my heart breaks for these children, their innocence stolen by their own parents, who sow seeds of fear and hatred in their minds.

We reach a section of the city where the east side of the street was recently opened to Palestinians. Several shops are open for businesses. A few people are out and about. A teenage Palestinian boy with a slender face and short gelled hair approaches me, selling beaded bracelets. I buy one from him for three shekels, less than one Canadian dollar. I am more intrigued by the message on the front of his brown t-shirt. In bright yellow are the words:

PEACE WILL COME, WHY NOT NOW.

"Where are you from?" he asks.

"Canada," I respond in Arabic. "I'm a member of the Arab-Jewish Women's Peace Coalition. We came to learn about what your life is like."

He smiles even wider and hands me another bracelet. "Take this one from me," he says.

"That's generous of you. Thank you," I agree not wanting to offend him. "I'll buy another one from you for my sister."

I want to stay a while and hear his story, but we have to move on. I forget to ask his name, but I will always remember his smile and optimism.

We come to another checkpoint blocking Shuhada Street from the south near the Ibrahimi Mosque, also known as the site of the Cave of the Patriarchs. This is *the* sacred place. Muslims named the mosque, which forms part of the site, in honour of Abraham. For Jews, this site is the second most sacred site in the world after Temple Mount/Noble Sanctuary in Jerusalem. Abraham is revered by all three of the world's monotheistic religions. According to the Book of Genesis, Abraham purchased this plot of land for a burial site. The location of the tombs is said to be the soul's doorway into heaven. All three religions claim that the subterranean caves beneath the structure contain the remains of Abraham and Sarah, Isaac and Rebecca, Jacob and Leah, and many others.

The structure has been used alternately as a mosque and church, depending on who occupied the land at the time, and who typically forbade the other from entering. Here, history repeats itself and the territorial imperative abounds. Today, the structure is part mosque, part synagogue with separate entrances for Jews and Muslims.

There are only two known access points to the caves beneath the enclosure. Every occupier tried to conceal these entrances, which are not accessible to the general public, out of respect for the dead. I would love to go inside, but it is not part of the tour. I think of my 87-year-old father. I am sure he would love to offer prayers here. He mentions Abraham five times a day when he prays.

I am roused from my reverie as the noon call to prayer rises from the speakers of a mosque to the south of me.

Allahu Akbar. God is great, reverberates twice over the hills of Hebron.

"I fired grenades into neighbourhoods for four months," Yehuda raises his voice to explain how his battalion made their presence felt in Hebron. "It was my first assignment. It felt like playing a video game. I'd spray cars with bullets, fire grenades, shoot at the school, shoot at water tanks."

Ashhadu an la ilaha illallah. I bear witness that there is no god but God (twice).

"I never beat up a Palestinian. I never slapped a Palestinian. But, I did use Palestinians as human shields."

Ashhadu anna Muhammad rasoul Allah. I bear witness Muhammad is God's messenger (twice).

"If we noticed a new car on the street, we'd crush it with our tanks. Kids throw stones. We use stun guns and tear gas, and then go back to the barracks for lunch. Our mission was posted on the walls of every barrack, 'to disrupt the daily routine of Palestinians.' That was our mission."

Hai ala salat. Hasten to worship (twice).

"If a soldier wants to watch a soccer match, he just goes into a house, locks the family in one room, watches the game and then he continues his operation. Some soldiers have killed Palestinians and afterwards took photos with the dead bodies."

He stops when he notices our bus pull up.

I admire his courage, the rawness of his honesty, admitting privately and publicly the things he inflicted on Palestinians, speaking the truth. It takes guts. No, more than that. It takes illumination and integrity, which Yehuda displays in abundance.

After the group settles into their seats on the bus, Yehuda opens up a big box and grabs an armful of books, soldier testimonies published by Breaking the Silence. He walks down the aisle passing them out.

"Any questions?" he asks, making his way to the front of the bus. I wait for a few seconds before raising my hand.

"Do women soldiers behave differently?"

"That's a good question," his face lights up. "You beat me to my next point. Our next book will be published in the upcoming months. It's a collection of testimonies from women soldiers."

I am surprised, but more disheartened to learn that women soldiers behaved no differently than the men. I had hoped, assumed incorrectly that as nurturers, women would somehow be innately more merciful.

Yehuda sits down and begins chatting with the bus driver. I stare out the window absorbed in thought. Hebron in Arabic is known as *Al-Khalil*, which means friend, in reference to Abraham. The Hebrew word for Hebron, *Hever*, also means friend. Sadly, I saw no signs of friendship in this "holy" place. How can friendships flourish here? There is agreement by Jews, Christians and Muslims that Hebron is sacred, the resting place of their common patriarchs and matriarchs. A pity though, there is little sanctity for the dead here and even less for the living. The daily lawlessness goes unpunished and rarely makes the mainstream evening news.

SIX

Handala:
An Iconic Activist

After the Wall around Rachel's Tomb was built, I felt terrible. Nobody was walking here, only the cats and dogs. The Wall creates a feeling...the feeling that it surrounds you; that you are not permitted to move. Every time, every day you see the Wall. When I look outside through the window to see the sunrise or sunset the Wall is in front of me. When I go to the Wall I feel that something closes in on my heart, as if the Wall is on my heart... When I see the Wall I also feel ashamed of myself, because it is created by human beings.

Melvina, THE WALL IS ON MY HEART
Poster hanging on the Wall in Bethlehem, 2011

We are dining at Abu Eli's restaurant in Bethlehem when I get my first chance to experience the Wall up close. As my Arab and Jewish sisters finish up their meals, I step outside to take photographs. I stand in front of Abu Eli's, staring at the three-story cement barrier across the street, blocking my view. To my right, the Wall follows the curved street out of sight. To my left, a block away, the road forks. There, two sections of the Wall converge at right angles, where a cement watchtower looms higher. Several metres of metal fencing run along the top and mounted cameras point downwards, covering all sides. It is both an awesome sight because of its sheer size and shocking to my small-town-Alberta eyes.

Israel began building the Wall in 2002. Two years later, the International

Court of Justice deemed it illegal under international law. But, its construction on private Palestinian land continued. It has several names, depending on which side of the Wall one lives. Israeli officials label it a "security fence," claiming that it is needed to keep suicide bombers out. Palestinians and others, including some Israeli activists, call it an "apartheid wall," a "land grab" and an "obstacle to peace."

When completed, the Wall will be over 700 kilometres in length, longer than the distance from Israel's most northern limits to its most southern point. It does not follow the Green Line, the pre-1967-war border between Israel and the Jordanian-controlled West Bank and the border between Israel and the Egyptian-controlled Gaza Strip. Much of the Wall was built well inside Palestinian territory, in many places just metres away from homes, schools, and businesses, annexing prime agricultural land and water resources on which thousands of Palestinians sustain themselves, turning villages into enclaves, separating people from their pastures and orchards, from each other, from their jobs, from their historical sites, schools and places of worship. Stealing livelihoods and sealing fates, the Wall literally imprisons Palestinians. Thousands are trapped in an area between the Wall and the Green Line known as, "No Man's Land."

In the urban areas like Bethlehem and other cities, towns and villages, the Wall is a concrete barrier eight metres high, crowned with coils of razor wire, embedded with armed watchtowers and checkpoints. Out in the rural areas, in the Occupied Palestinian Territories, the Wall is an electrified, razor-wire barrier, three metres high with 100-metre buffer zones on either side of it, together with military patrol roads, trenches, cameras and sensors. The Wall cannot be willed away or ignored. It reminds Palestinians daily that they live in a prison. Like a prison, the Wall serves the same purpose of isolating and controlling people, leaving little room to think of anything else.

I want to cross the street, get up close where I can see more of the graffiti on the Wall, but I am nervous about the Israeli soldiers in the watchtower. I cannot see them, but I know they are up there in their cupola watching every moving thing. Our waiter, Amjad, comes outside while I am still mulling over what to do. He lights a cigarette.

"Would you like one?" he asks, holding the package out to me.

His ink-black hair is curly and cropped short, contrasting his chiselled face and dark eyes.

"*Shukran,*" I reply, which makes him smile. I've found my fluency in Arabic has opened up doors, put people at ease when they realize that this trip is more to me than a vacation to the Holy Land.

With a chuckle, Amjad tells me, "I thought you were the Jew and the lady sitting to your left the Arab."

"*En Jad?* For real?" I ask, chuckling.

"For real. I am happy you can understand me," he says. "What do you do in Canada?"

"I write and edit communications for the government."

"I would like to go to Italy or Canada," he tells me, puffing on his cigarette. "I have no future here. Tourists used to come regularly to Bethlehem, but the Wall has killed tourism and the economy."

It occurs to me that only one car had driven past since I have been standing here. The Wall has diverted traffic away from the businesses along this street.

Amjad says, "Hundreds of businesses were forced to close. Parts of the city have become ghettos."

Our conversation hits a pause while what he has said sinks in.

What am I missing here? This is the birthplace of Jesus, the Prince of Peace, revered by billions around the world. How can such desecration be tolerated?

"I want to photograph the graffiti on the Wall. Will that be a problem?" I ask, gesturing at the watchtower.

Amjad smiles. "It's no big deal. Follow me."

He crushes out his cigarette and starts walking north with me trailing. At the end of the block we cross an east-west street and approach the Wall.

Standing at its base, the Wall seems even larger. Its immensity amplifies my sense of powerlessness. Its grey dreariness is offset with colourful artwork left by professional artists, serving as metaphors that cross language barriers, and with graffiti in multiple languages: French, Italian, German, Arabic and Spanish. I am intrigued by all the markings left by locals and internationals from around the world, initials and dates, mushy notes, famous people quotes and crude drawings. The Wall has become a political commentary on Israel's treatment of the Palestinians.

PLANT JUSTICE. HARVEST PEACE.

HERE IS A WALL AT WHICH TO WEEP.

FORGIVE US FATHER.

I HAVE A DREAM. THIS IS NOT PART OF THAT DREAM.

One line of graffiti captivates me:

NOW THAT I HAVE SEEN, I AM RESPONSIBLE.

This message echoes in my head, as if aimed directly at me. A voice within nags, "What are you going to do now that you have seen?"

I walk west 30 metres along the base of the Wall, snapping photographs of the graffiti. Amjad stays close, stopping when I stop, walking when I walk.

"I had hoped to come across a Bansky mural," I say to him as we retrace our steps back.

Bansky, a British graffiti artist, is well known to Palestinians for the murals he painted on the Wall in the Occupied Palestinian Territories; they highlight the reality and inhumanity of the Wall. Escape is a common theme in Bansky's murals: a little boy painting a ladder up the Wall, a little girl being swept over the Wall by a bunch of balloons, people riding up an escalator to the top of the Wall.

"My favourite Bansky mural," I think out loud, "is the one of a little girl in a dress patting down a soldier."

Amjad's dimples emerge.

"Someone painted a copy of it on a wall leading out of Bethlehem," he gestures north. "I know a few taxi drivers who now offer graffiti tours in the occupied territories. Some tourists hire them to drive around so they can see Bansky's murals."

"May I take your photograph next the Wall?"

Amjad is happy to pose as I snap a couple of photographs. I check my watch. I have about ten minutes before our driver picks us up for our next destination, the Church of the Nativity, so I quickly take photographs of the Wall without reading all the layers of graffiti.

One simple drawing catches my eye: a cartoon of a little boy. I gaze at him. Sparse, spiky hair, barefoot, with his back to the world, hands clasped behind his back, he stands in silent opposition to the Wall and pulls at me. I know who he is. This cartoon is not some random drawing.

His name is Handala. He is a 10-year-old Palestinian refugee, who appears on t-shirts, posters and is drawn on the Wall throughout the Occupied Palestinian Territories, a constant reminder. He is faceless, yet *is* the face of millions of Palestinian refugees who want nothing more than to return home. Some renditions show Handala with his back turned, urinating on the Wall.

Naji Al-Ali, a Palestinian cartoonist, created Handala in 1975; it became his signature cartoon. The cartoonist became a refugee at the age of 10, forced out of his home and village when the State of Israel was created. He grew up in a refugee camp in Lebanon. On Al-Ali's website, www.handala.org, the cartoonist explained the story behind Handala:

> I present him to the poor and named him Handala as a symbol of our bitterness. I drew him as a child who is not beautiful. His hair is like the hair of a hedgehog who uses his thorns as a weapon. Handala is not a fat, happy, relaxed or pampered child. He is barefoot like the refugee camp children ... Even though he is rough, he smells of amber. His hands are clasped behind his back as a sign of rejection at a time when solutions are presented to us the American way.

It hit me hard when I learned that Naji Al-Ali, the creator of Handala, has been dead for more than two decades. He was assassinated in 1987 in London, outside the office of a Kuwaiti newspaper where he worked creating political cartoons. He was only 50. His murder remains unsolved.

On his website, Al-Ali described Handala's uniqueness, "The laws of nature do not apply to him. He will stay a 10-year-old until he can return home."

When I notice our bus pulling up in front of the restaurant a block away, I put my camera away. As Amjad and I cross the street in silence, I think about the types of cartoons Al-Ali might have created if he was still alive today. Daily life for Palestinians has only gotten worse. Israel began building the Wall early in the new millennia, more than 20 years after his death.

Israel's military occupation and colonization of Palestine has continued. Peace talks were just that, *talk*. *Kalam farigh*, empty words, as my father would say. Nobel Peace Prizes were doled out to leaders on both sides yet peace has not come to fruition. Meanwhile, another *dunam* of fertile land is being bulldozed, another ancient olive grove is being uprooted, another home is being demolished, another hilltop is being usurped for illegal Jewish settlements, another checkpoint and watchtower is being constructed, another exclusively Jewish-only road is being paved, another segment of the Wall is going up. Meanwhile, another Palestinian family goes hungry, another ghetto is created. Another Palestinian child is born, who, like Handala, will have his childhood stolen and his life stalled. I would not blame him if he grows up with his back turned to a world where sanity has been suspended, where home is one big open-air prison.

"Thank you for walking with me," I say to Amjad.

"*Bissalaama*, go in peace," he answers, and heads inside the restaurant.

Pity too few people know about Handala, I lament to myself back on the bus as I scan through the saved images on my camera that I took of the Wall.

Pity too few people know about this Wall.

I try to think positively as we near the Church of the Nativity. The Berlin Wall was eventually brought down, bit by bit. I pray the same thing happens here.

In the meantime, Handala, whose name in Arabic means "medicinal bitter desert fruit," will continue to symbolize the struggle for freedom—still a refugee like millions of Palestinians, still dispossessed and oppressed after more than 60 years. Handala will remain an omnipresent image on the Wall and the walls of homes, on t-shirts and the insides of university lockers, a reminder of humanity's universal right to return home enshrined in international law. He will stay—for as long as the Wall is standing.

SEVEN

Dawn at Qalandia Checkpoint

By our very presence at the checkpoints, we are saying 'NO to the checkpoints. NO to the Occupation.'
Ronny Pearlman, Machsom Watch, *2009*

I t is still dark outside when we leave the Oasis of Peace. By 5:00 AM, our bus is winding its way down from the hillock where the village is located. All I can see out the window is my own expression, unreadable as the passing landscape. It's hard to know how to feel about all the things I've seen.

Our group sits quietly as our driver heads east on Highway 3, and then north on Highway 443 through rolling hills towards Ramallah. Our destination is Qalandia checkpoint, located between Jerusalem and Ramallah, the biggest checkpoint in the West Bank — one of more than 600 Israeli-imposed roadblocks, many of which are permanent installations.

I stare at my reflection, feeling strangely blessed. I know many Palestinians back home in Edmonton, who have been barred by Israel from returning to their homes and villages, even to visit, would give anything to be in my place. Every day so far has been an adventure, a learning experience, an opportunity to meet Israeli and Palestinian peace activists, whose tireless efforts are rarely reported. I want to tell the world about them and shatter some of the myths about what is happening in the Holy Land. I am also anxious thinking about what might happen while witnessing the dawn exodus at

Qalandia checkpoint, having read about the long line-ups, the indignity and humiliation, and horrific accounts of violence that often occur.

About half an hour later our driver stops to let us out. He cannot go any further because the road is blocked by the Wall and checkpoint. It feels surreal, as if I have been dropped off in a foreboding world of colossal concrete walls and watchtowers — a setting conjured up by an imaginative fiction writer. The Wall slices through the landscape, dwarfing everything in the grey dawn. An even higher cement watchtower stands menacingly. And, for added security, there is a metal fence about three metres high at the edge of a buffer zone that runs parallel to the wall. I'm guessing it's electrified.

Vehicles are lined up as far as I can see. Only those with Israeli-issued license plates will be allowed through the checkpoint. The only other way to traverse the barrier is on foot. Not all Palestinians will be allowed to cross, only those with Israeli-issued permits, ID cards or magnetic cards. No one waits at the west-facing entrance or Jerusalem side of the checkpoint. At this time of the day, Palestinians will line up at the east entrance, on the Ramallah side, trying to head for Jerusalem, the opposite direction from where we are going.

Noor leads the way to the west-facing entrance of the terminal. We follow close, like a row of ducklings trailing their mother to water. I know we are being watched by hidden cameras. We crossed Qalandia checkpoint before and other checkpoints during our journey, but not at dawn.

It only takes a few minutes for the nine of us to go through the steel turnstiles, metal detector and X-ray machine. The Israeli soldier behind the barred enclosure barely looks up at me as I flash my Canadian passport. Ronny Pearlman, a human rights activist and member of Machsom Watch, is waiting for us on the other side. She is a youthful-looking grandmother, with vivid green eyes and short, light brown hair. A name tag is pinned to the neckline of her shirt; it has a black eye in the top left corner, her group's logo. We gather around her, exchanging greetings and introductions.

"Machsom is the Hebrew word meaning 'checkpoint,'" Ronny explains.

Machsom Watch was established in 2001 and is comprised of over 350 Israeli Jews, all women, mostly middle-aged and older. They take turns twice a day at the major checkpoints in the West Bank, volunteering in shifts that last up to five hours. The group's objectives are to protest the existence of the checkpoints and the occupation of Palestinian lands by Israel, to monitor and document incidents and soldier conduct and abuse, and to intervene on behalf of Palestinians when they are being denied access to cross.

Qalandia checkpoint looks like a border crossing or bus terminal, minus any amenities and niceties like toilets, water fountains and food venues. Nice doesn't live here. The complex is made of metal pillars and has a roof of corrugated iron; the interior is a maze of blue and grey metal corridors and cages. At the end of the cage-like corridors are turnstiles controlled by a soldier who is hidden from view in a cubicle, and with a press of a button allows one person at a time to cross. Past the turnstiles, there is another line where Palestinians must pass through X-ray machines and metal detectors before showing their paperwork to a soldier in a glass cubicle.

A crowd of men, hundreds, fans out beyond the entrance of the terminal on the Ramallah side. The turnstiles are not open yet. I stare in disbelief as the men at the front of the crowd are queuing in lines. I wonder how long they have been waiting, and begin feeling claustrophobic by the sight of the ones at the front of the line, completely caged, inside three, side-by-side, narrow corridors about 10 metres long, made of grey metal beams, corridors so narrow a pudgy Palestinian would have to stand sideways. Even the tops of the corridors have metal bars. Overkill. What was its architect thinking and trying to prevent? These cages are specifically designed for humans; but, they remind me of coops I have seen on farms and cattle ranches. They also remind me of animal cages found in zoos and transport me back to when I was 10 years old, feeling sad and having the urge to unlock all the birdcages during my first visit to a zoo.

Some of the men have their hands in their pockets and look at me with eyes that seem to say, "What's the point?" Others hang on to the bars and some lean on them for support. I try not to gawk. I am embarrassed somehow and can't look them in the eye. I feel guilty. As a Canadian, I have the freedom to move unencumbered in Israel and the Occupied Palestinian Territories, but the indigenous Palestinian people do not enjoy this fundamental right.

Their eyes, sombre and seemingly resigned yet undefeated, will always haunt me.

I begin to feel nauseous and take a few deep breaths. I get a whiff of coffee and look around, thinking perhaps I had imagined it. Then I spot a medium-built man with grey hair near the entrance, selling it. I watch in admiration at his resourcefulness as he dispenses Arabic coffee into a mini-size paper cups from a stainless steel urn sitting on a round, plastic table off to one side. Several men are gathered around him, waiting to buy a cup. I am tempted by the aroma and reminded that I have not had my morning coffee.

The quietness is jolting. Despite the harshness and humiliation, or perhaps in spite of it, the men wait patiently and calmly in their queues. What choice do they have but to submit to Israel's military might? I wonder how people in Canada would react. I've witnessed people back home lose their temper in traffic or because they spent a few minutes waiting in line at a bank, grocery store or Tim Horton's. I wonder how patient and calm I would be if I was forced to spend several hours, every day on the way to work—just to cross an area about a block long.

What would I do if I had to go to the washroom?

Some of the men watch us. A few are wearing suits; many are dressed in jeans and t-shirts and carry plastic bags. I assume it's their lunch.

"The Palestinians are surrounded by Israeli settlements and outposts, yet the Israelis say, 'We are surrounded by hostile Palestinians,'" Ronny tells us. "I've been coming here once a week for the past eight years. After our shifts, we write reports. Some of us have made films and posted them on *YouTube*. Our job is to report to the world, to be a living, concrete opposition to the Occupation. We aren't just nice ladies. I have so much empathy. The Palestinians live hard lives."

According to Machsom Watch, checkpoints, walls and other barriers rupture the basic fabric of life in the Occupied Palestinian Territories. Access to medical services, schools and universities, and places of work, worship and commerce are severely restricted. Palestinians are barred from their land and families are prevented from visiting each other. The growing network of walls, barriers and checkpoints has devastated the economy and led to a rise in poverty, unemployment, illness and malnutrition.

In June 2004, the World Bank Press reported that these barriers have caused the Palestinian people to suffer "one of the worst recessions in modern history."

Permission to cross is often arbitrary and at the whim of a pubescent-looking Israeli soldier at the checkpoint. I've read numerous reports of ambulances carrying the sick or injured that were prevented from crossing, pregnant women delivering their babies at checkpoints, newborns and their mothers dying because they were denied access to hospitals. Israeli soldiers have shot at, detained, injured or harassed children on their way to school; they have been known to even close schools arbitrarily.

Again, I find myself comparing this place to Canada. A woman who died because she was denied access to a hospital would be in the headlines for days. There would be an inquest, a media expose, nationwide political debate on how to prevent such a thing from happening again. Here, the silence continues while people are herded like cattle, staring forward and waiting in lines.

Ronny leads us around the back of the crowd to a waiting area. There are rows of burgundy-painted, metal-meshed benches bolted to the floor. No one is sitting here. We congregate around her.

"Few Palestinians use the seats," she says. "They prefer to stand for hours while they wait, out of fear of losing their place in line."

The men's eyes follow us, I presume because we are something new to observe. Many would have seen Ronny at the checkpoint before and know she is there to advocate and help them if needed. She is also a window into a world invisible to most. I want to take some photographs, but feel uncomfortable aiming my camera at the men. I snap a few nonetheless. They do not appear to mind.

Ronny teaches us the "ABCs of the Occupation," while keeping one eye on us and the other on the crowds trying to cross the checkpoint.

"Checkpoints prevent Palestinians from being human beings," she tells us. "They wait like this every day for hours. Many can't pass. More than 200,000 Palestinians are prevented from entering Israel, and they'll never know why. The army is busy fighting the enemy. Now they want to give the checkpoints over to private companies, to be managed by mercenaries. There are already two privately run checkpoints in the West Bank.

"The rules keep changing, 'Today, only five pita bread can be taken across.' Many Palestinians are not allowed to take cooked food for lunch. They have to wake up very early and stand in line for hours then go work all day, some of them in the fields. They need to eat."

As Ronny talks, I glance at some of the men. Some look back, stone-faced; others appear half-asleep, possibly because they have been up since three in the morning to get here. Some half-smile, perhaps hopeful that when I go back home I might show their photographs and tell my family and friends what life is like for them. I am baffled by how the extraordinary has become so ordinary.

"There was a Palestinian man who used to cross Qalandia three times a week to take his 10-year-old son to a hospital in Jerusalem for dialysis," Ronny informs us. "One morning he was prevented from crossing the checkpoint, with no explanation. The man was forced to arrange for someone else to take his son to the hospital for treatment."

Ronny explains that Israeli soldiers use this strategy to recruit informants. Palestinians know what it means when a soldier asks, for example, "Do you want to go with your son to the hospital?" Many Palestinians are forced to make painful, unbearable choices, medical help for your sick child in exchange for spying and reporting on family, friends or fellow villagers. It is a predicament; someone will suffer, regardless of what the Palestinian chooses.

It is seven o'clock when the turnstiles finally open. I hear the clicking and clanging of metal as the crowd moves through, one at a time to another queue on the other side. Teenagers clutching mobile phones begin arriving, as do children in school uniforms carrying backpacks painted with Batman and Barbie, and more men, women with babies, and elderly grandmothers and grandfathers.

Noor taps me on the shoulder and points out a mother and her young daughter sitting on one of the benches behind us. The little girl appears to be about six years old. Her shoulder-length hair is pulled back from her face by a pink hair band, framing her big, brown eyes. She is sandwiched between a backpack and her mother, who is reading her a book. In her world, going to school with armed soldiers controlling your every movement is normal. I point my camera at them and snap a photograph. The little girl squirms in agitation and complains to her mother. Without looking up to see who took their photograph, the mother tries to divert her daughter's attention back to the book. I feel bad for intruding.

Qalandia Checkpoint has a "Humanitarian Gate." But, it is not open yet, even though it is now after eight o'clock. Students on their way to school and others wait in a corridor of metal bars leading to the south-facing gate. Ronny notices the growing line-up and excuses herself to make a phone call, I assume to enquire why the gate is not open.

Soon, an elderly woman with cheerless blue eyes arrives at the checkpoint. She appears to be ill and is being supported on either side, I presume, by her adult children. Ronny's watchful eye spots them and she is on her phone again. We follow her as she walks over to the Humanitarian Gate to talk to the commander of the checkpoint. I assume he is there because of her call. A wall of blue metal bars separates her from him. The commander, over six feet tall with an M16 slung over his shoulders, towers over the petite grandmother, who stands a full foot shorter. With trepidation, I shoot a couple photographs. He smiles respectfully at Ronny as he speaks to her in Hebrew. Finally, after additional questions and answers, he allows the sick, elderly woman and others who have been waiting to pass through the gate, where they show their IDs to a policeman in a two-toned blue uniform. The elderly woman glances back at Ronny as if to let her know she is grateful for the intervention.

It is difficult to process the scene. The sun shines through the bars, casting long shadows on the tiled floor. Numb, I gaze at people through the openings between the bars as they shuffle through more halls of metal and concrete, stopping again to show their paperwork to another soldier.

Ronny continues talking to the commander. I move in closer, not hearing her question, but only his response in English.

"They will fight," he tells her with a nervous laugh.

"They wait like this morning and afternoon. It's sadism. *That* will push the Palestinians to violence," Ronny replies with a calm feistiness.

It seems reasonable to think tempers would flare under such conditions. I turn away, muttering an Arabic profanity, which I have no doubt the commander understands, surprised by my immediate reaction, but I do not care nor do I feel shame. Care and shame do not live here either. I keep asking myself, "How can the world allow this human suffering and indignity to continue?"

The commander walks away without responding.

Ronny tells us, "Israel has zero intention of leaving the West Bank and managing the situation. There's zero motivation to coexist. Israel's practice is to pretend the Palestinians don't exist. The bottom line: if Palestinians, for instance, travel to Germany to study, they lose their status. They become stateless. The world won't stop Israel. The West tolerates this. Palestinians think the whole world is against them, except for some of the rich Arab states."

I can't imagine how utterly lonely that must be.

It takes several hours for the crowd to thin. Over 4,000 people crossed Qalandia checkpoint this morning. It is now almost 11 o'clock. We leave the waiting area and walk outside the terminal. Every person crossing the checkpoint from the Ramallah side is greeted with three yellow signs as they enter the terminal—a welcome and a warning in three languages: English, Hebrew and Arabic. The English version reads:

WELCOME TO "ATAROT" CHECKPOINT
- YOU ARE NOW ENTERING A MILITARY AREA. TO MAKE YOUR TRANSIT EASY AND TO AVOID UNNECESSARY DELAY FIRST READ THESE INSTRUCTIONS AND THEN OBEY THEM.
- DO NOT ENTER CARRYING ARTICLES MADE OF METAL OR OBJECTS DECLARED FORBIDDEN BY THE AUTHORITY.
- PREPARE YOUR DOCUMENTS FOR INSPECTION.
- YOUR DOCUMENTS MUST BE PRESENTED AT EACH INSPECTION POINT.
- COATS MUST BE REMOVED.
- PERSONS REFUSING TO FOLLOW INSPECTION OR SIGN-POSTED INSTRUCTION WILL NOT BE PERMITTED TO COMPLETE THEIR TRANSIT.
- WE WISH YOU A SAFE AND PLEASANT TRANSIT.
- MAY YOU GO IN PEACE AND RETURN IN PEACE.

I re-read the last two lines. They are familiar expressions, but here the irony is difficult to brush off. The sweet words taunt me. As we prepare to leave, three pigeons fly in and peck at the ground near our feet.

"Luckily, they have wings," I say, thinking out loud.

Ronny smiles, "My son is an ornithologist."

I cannot resist asking her, "What does your son think of your volunteer work as an advocate and a voice for Palestinians?"

"He doesn't agree with me," she replies without emotion. "He says, 'Everyone hates us. Everyone wants to throw us into the sea.'"

I want to know how she feels about this. I want Ronny to share some examples of how this disagreement manifests itself, how she deals with it, but she does not elaborate further.

This morning, I witnessed how thousands of Palestinians start their day. I saw what the absence of freedom looks like, and sense the experience at Qalandia checkpoint will change me in ways I do not yet fully grasp. I realize just how much I had taken for granted my freedom to move about as needed and wanted.

Still, it is comforting to know there are caring, heroic Jewish women like Ronny. She speaks seven languages and though she is opposed to the Occupation, she still considers herself a loyal citizen of Israel. Undeterred by the opinions of immediate family members, she places herself in harm's way as a human shield, advocating for Palestinian freedom, challenging Israel's army, a watchful eye at major checkpoints every day, twice a day, in key locations throughout the Occupied Palestinian Territories.

EIGHT

Yad Vashem: "Never Again"?

The original founders of the Jewish state could surely not imagine
the irony facing Israel today: in escaping the ashes of the Holocaust,
they have incarcerated another people in a hell similar in its nature
– though not its extent – to the Warsaw ghetto.
Oona King, The Guardian, *June 12, 2003*

A biblical line greets visitors. It is carved into the top of a concrete
gateway at the entrance to Yad Vashem. It reads:

I WILL PUT MY BREATH INTO YOU AND

YOU SHALL LIVE AGAIN, AND I WILL SET YOU

UPON YOUR OWN SOIL.

We are about to tour a 45-acre Holocaust museum built on a mountaintop
at the western outskirts of Jerusalem. Established in 1953, five years after the
creation of the State of Israel, this museum commemorates the millions of
Jewish people murdered by the Nazis and pays tribute to the people who
worked to save the lives of European Jews.

But not all of us want to be here.

"I'm not comfortable," Zubaida, one of the Arab sisters, told the group
yesterday at our debriefing. "It's hard to keep hearing about the Holocaust
while for the past six decades the world has failed to see and stop Israel's
oppression of Palestinians."

She joins three of the Jewish sisters, who have visited Yad Vashem before; they stay behind at the visitor's center near the entrance, where there is a bookstore, resource area and cafeteria, and do their own thing.

I team up with Noor, Alimah, Ester and Shai. I've never been to a Holocaust museum, and during our planning meetings, I jumped at the chance to visit Yad Vashem. I wanted to learn and pay tribute to the victims of the Holocaust. But, now I feel ambivalent as my brother's words flash through my mind. One month before our journey, I was sharing the coalition's itinerary with him, listing off some of the places we planned to visit: Jericho, Hebron, Bethlehem, Ramallah, Sderot and Yad Vashem.

"Yad Vashem? Do you realize where Yad Vashem is built?" he asked in exasperation. Before I could answer, "No," he left the room and came back with a book, *Remembering Deir Yassin: The Future of Israel and Palestine*, which he insisted I read before coming to the Holy Land.

"Tell them about the massacre in Deir Yassin," he reminded me when we said goodbye later that evening. "There's no memorial, not even a marker to commemorate the Palestinian victims."

Deir Yassin massacre occurred in the spring of 1948, one month before the creation of the State of Israel. The village was located outside the area the United Nations sanctioned for an Israeli state. In the middle of the night, members of the Stern and Irgun gangs, armed Zionist militias, broke into homes and murdered over 100 Palestinians in Deir Yassin. The gangs rounded up some of the men, paraded them through Jerusalem and later shot them in a stone quarry. They forced some families into cargo trucks and drove them away from the village. They loaded 55 orphaned children onto a bus and dumped them off on a Jerusalem street corner, near the Church of the Holy Sepulchre. Hind al-Husseini, a Palestinian woman from a prominent family in Jerusalem, rescued them, converting her grandfather's mansion where she was born into an orphanage and later a school. One of the Irgun gang members, Menachem Begin, would later become the Prime Minister of Israel and a Nobel Peace Prize Laureate.

Jewish militias depopulated the village of its Palestinian inhabitants, scattering the surviving 750 villagers into the Diaspora. They spared most of the homes and later populated them with Jewish immigrants from Europe. History denied. Israel literally erased Deir Yassin from the map, like hundreds of other Palestinian villages, as if they had never existed.

Today, the former village of Deir Yassin is home to the Kfar Shaul Mental Health Center, a facility Israel built for pilgrims and tourists, who come to the Holy Land only to develop the Jerusalem Syndrome, a temporary psychiatric condition where some visitors, Jews, Christians and Muslims, are so overwhelmed with the Holy Land, they become delusional and begin to believe they are Jesus, the Virgin Mary, John the Baptist or some other religious figure on a divine mission.

I knew that this massacre was the start of the Palestinian Diaspora. But, I had no idea until I read the book from my brother that Yad Vashem was built on a mountaintop overlooking what remains of Deir Yassin. Two horrors so close together, one is immortalized, the other all but obliterated.

I have to wonder if any of my Jewish and Arab sisters know of this. Not wanting to detract from my first experience touring a Holocaust museum, and even though I also want the group to pay tribute to the victims of Deir Yassin, I decide to wait for a more opportune time to mention anything.

I tell myself, "For now, forget Deir Yassin. Forget the experience at Qalandia checkpoint earlier this morning and forget Israel's occupation of Palestinians. For now, experience Yad Vashem. Just focus on the victims of the Holocaust."

I know this site is important to my Jewish sisters. We spent many meetings discussing which places the group would visit.

"Balance," was an often repeated plea by some of them, the need to balance the number of Jewish places we would visit with Palestinian ones.

"I agree," I always added. It was the fair and right thing to do.

We begin outside, walking in dappled light along the Avenue of the Righteous Among Nations, a wide stone path lined on both sides by trees. These trees were planted to honour non-Jews: Christians, Muslims and others who risked their lives during the Holocaust to save the lives of Jewish people. I pause to read some of the names and their countries of origin inscribed on plaques placed under the trees. I'm not surprised and it is heart-warming to learn Muslims also helped.

The walkway leads visitors to the entrance of the Holocaust History Museum, the main memorial within Yad Vashem's multi-complex site. Covering an area of over 4,200 square metres, the entrance and exit of the 180-metre-long, triangular structure, protrude out of the mountainsides. Constructed mostly underground, the museum's uppermost edge is a skylight. Inside, visitors experience the story of the Holocaust chronologically; each of the 10 exhibition galleries is devoted to one of its dark chapters.

It is dim inside, the mood, sombre. The halls are crowded with people. I am overwhelmed with emotions as we zigzag from one exhibition hall to the next. Shai stays close to me the whole time; we remain silent. As if in my own bubble, I read posters detailing historical accounts, personal stories and journal entries. I read letters to family members, letters thrown from trains while en route to concentration camps, a greeting card hidden in a loaf of bread to Sonia from her mother and sister. I read disturbing quotations and philosophical ones and record a few:

> I know that when I stand before God on Judgement Day, I shall not be asked the question posed to Cain — where were you when your brother's blood was crying out to God.
>
> *Imre Bathory, Hungary*

> My name is 174517...we will carry the tattoo on our left arm until we die.
>
> *Primo Levi*

> They came for the communist, and I did not object for I was not a communist. They came for the socialist, and I did not object for I was not a socialist. They came for the Jew, and I did not object for I was not a Jew. When they came for me, there was no one left.
>
> *Martin Niemöller, German pastor*

Farther on, I gaze at the artwork and walls of photographs of people who perished, black and white and sepia-toned. Family portraits. Photographs of mass executions as they are being carried out. Piles of dead bodies, naked women being herded to death camps, emaciated children dressed in rags sitting on a ghetto curb, a mother with her back turned to shield her child from an unseen executioner. I listen to heart-wrenching video testimonies of survivors and observe personal artefacts encased behind glass: diaries, combs and rusted spoons.

I feel numb, dissociated from my body, unable to control the silent springs percolating up from the depths of my soul and streaming down my face unabashed.

Some artefacts are especially painful to observe and will remain imprinted in my mind, like the collection of shoes belonging to Holocaust victims, black and brown ones, children's shoes, and adult shoes, hundreds are inset in the floor of one exhibition hall and covered in glass that is flush with the floor. And the photographs of the 800-kilometre women's death march, photographs of Jewish people behind metal bars, skeletal, eyes sunken and wide, terrified. And metal instruments, which the Nazis used to measure the breadth of a person's nose to determine the extent of their inferiority or degree of Jewishness. I can't help but wonder if Hitler's extermination policy had applied to Arabs, the other Semites.

Yet, as I try, I can't stop Israel's dispossession and occupation of the Palestinians from flickering through my mind. Some of the displays actually serve to remind me. It is difficult not to notice the parallels between Nazi lies, propaganda and racist rhetoric, which enabled the Holocaust, and Israel's lies, propaganda and racist rhetoric, which facilitated the ethnic cleansing of Palestinians from their land in 1948 to create a Jewish state, and its ongoing propaganda, which enables and perpetuates the Occupation. It is not so easy to push aside these thoughts as I read posters laced with Hitler's propaganda, which poisoned otherwise ordinary people into believing in the inferiority of the Jewish people, and other undesirables, viewing them as sub-human, which seems to have made it possible and easier to carry out mass murder.

In his lexicon of hate, *Mein Kampf,* Hitler wrote:

> No one need be surprised if among our people the personification of the devil, as the symbol of all evil, assumes the living shape of the Jews.

It is all too much to fathom, the scale of Hitler's murder campaign, the voices of survivors, the journal entries of victims, their photographs and artefacts.

We emerge from the dimness of the Holocaust History Museum onto a large balcony. I welcome the fresh air and bright afternoon sun. Before me is a stunning panoramic view of verdant valleys and hills. I try to get my bearings, scanning the opposite slopes for Deir Yassin, trying to recall the details of a map I studied on-line showing the location of this former village in relation to Yad Vashem. I am quite certain it is north of this point and take a few photographs so that I can examine them later. I am probably looking right at it, but I am unable to distinguish Deir Yassin from other development nestled amidst the forested slopes.

The dwindling number of the survivors and their descendants continue to be barred from ever returning or even visiting Deir Yassin. They remain haunted by bittersweet memories of a more peaceful past. The olive trees they planted, nurtured and named after family members, the *ein*, where the women congregated to draw water and socialize, the sunny courtyards where they dried grapes and figs, the breezy rooftops where they slept in the summer under a starry firmament, the herb gardens of oregano, mint and lemon verbena, the mosque, the cemetery—are all gone.

The ghosts of Deir Yassin continue to cry out on the opposite slopes, invisible to unknowing visitors to Yad Vashem. There is no memorial to honour them. Israeli officials have barred the placement of a simple plaque, even after repeated requests by displaced survivors and their families. I cannot equate the Holocaust to the massacre at Deir Yassin. The two dark chapters in history are not comparable. Thankfully, the Holocaust ended, but the fact is that Israeli's occupation continues and the Palestinians remain as they have been described, "Victims of the victim." The suffering of both victims deserves commemoration. I silently recite the *fatiha*, the opening chapter of the Qur'an, for the victims of the Holocaust and for the victims of Deir Yassin.

There is much to see. One could easily spend an entire day in Yad Vashem, and more. We stop for a few moments at the Hall of Remembrance, a low concrete building, dim and empty except for the eternal flame burning. The floor is black basalt and engraved with the names of concentration camps and killing sites. We also walk through the grounds taking in the outdoor exhibits, sculptures and memorials, making our way past the Pillar of Heroism to the Children's Memorial, an area dug into an underground cavern. The inside is blackened and festooned with memorial candles, a Jewish tradition in remembrance of the dead. Mirrors reflect the flickering candles, creating the illusion of an inky sky twinkling with stars. As we slowly walk through, a recorded voice reads out the names, ages and nationalities of the approximately 1.5 million Jewish children massacred by the Nazis. It is more than any of us can bear. We all break down.

The layout and architecture of Yad Vashem are brilliant and unique. I am thankful for the opportunity to visit this important memorial, but Yad Vashem is also one of the most humbling and heartbreaking places I have visited in the Holy Land. After spending most of the afternoon here, I'm emotionally spent and feel a profound loss I can't articulate. I have the urge to run away, unable to understand the madness involved in systematically exterminating Jewish people or any other people. The past, it seems, is not for learning from, but for repeating. Yad Vashem's message, "Never to forget man's inhumanity to man," provides a modicum of hope, but I am saddened by the knowledge that this promise does not apply to Palestinians. In this moment, as we crowd into three waiting cabs, I'm ashamed of being human and want to relinquish my humanity. I feel like morphing into something more merciful, nobler, like a cat, or a dog.

NINE

Now it is Real: Now What?

If you don't read the newspaper, you are uninformed; if you do read the newspaper, you are misinformed.

Mark Twain

Back home, familiar surroundings seem strange at first. I do not know how long I have been standing motionless in front of one of my bookcases, my eyes roaming over the rows of books. Books by Kahlil Gibran, Naguib Mahfouz, Mahmoud Darwish and Hanan al-Shaykh gape back at me. They are exactly as I left them, organized somewhat according to subject matter and author, but it is as though I am looking at them for the first time.

Everything looks different now.

It has been a week. I am trying to resume my normal life, but I feel discombobulated, in need it seems of therapy to help process what I witnessed and heard. Melancholy persists. I came back armed with new information, having learned many things, yet I feel as if I no longer understand the world.

Visiting the Holy Land felt like going home. A part of me remains there, lingering in the alleys of the Old City, the hills of Hebron and the ancient souks in Haifa and Jaffa. It felt like meeting family, only these family members live behind concrete walls and face armed soldiers and settlers every day. I am consumed with guilt as I commute to and from work, my route free of obstacles, harm and humiliation, while thousands of people in the Occupied Palestinian Territories are lined up, awaiting their fate at an Israeli checkpoint. I realize how much I had taken my freedom of mobility for granted. Seldom did I consider the ease of being able to just get into my car and go wherever I please or need.

Mostly, I cannot shake the thought, *What Palestine?* I have just witnessed a vanishing Palestine, an imprisoned Palestine. Somewhere in the Occupied Palestinian Territories right now, another home is being demolished, another olive grove is being destroyed, another teenager is being arrested and tortured for allegedly throwing stones, and another hilltop is being seized to expand the State of Israel. It's sobering and saddens me to admit I have less hope now after my journey. The chances for the creation of a Palestinian state and chances for peace appear slim and likely will not come to fruition in my lifetime; perhaps not even in my children's lifetime; perhaps never.

I detest myself for feeling this way.

Still, what resonates is knowing not all Israelis support their government's military occupation and dispossession of Palestinians. I met Israeli Jews who volunteer their time raising awareness about the Occupation, assisting Palestinians, going against family and friends and putting themselves in harm's way by advocating for human rights. I want to tell as many people as I can about groups like Breaking the Silence, Machsom Watch and The Other Voice. I realize that there will be no peace for me, until I do so. I am dogged by a line of graffiti on the Wall near Bethlehem:

NOW THAT I HAVE SEEN, I AM RESPONSIBLE.

Less than two weeks after the Arab Jewish Women's Peace Coalition's journey through Israel and Palestine, I am at home, watching the November 9, 2009, *CBC News.* Western leaders have gathered in Germany to celebrate the 20th anniversary of the dismantling of the Berlin Wall. These leaders praise those who helped bring it down. They talk about equality, human rights and freedoms, give themselves standing ovations and smile for the cameras.

"Freedom and equality depend on your religion or ethnicity," I say to the television. "Freedom depends on which side of the wall you're living on."

Not one leader mentions the continued Israeli subjugation of Palestinians. Not one leader speaks out against the illegal and immoral wall imprisoning Palestinian communities—which, when completed, will be over 700 kilometres long, three times longer than the Berlin Wall.

The journey brought the nine of us members of the Arab Jewish Women's Peace Coalition closer together. We returned from the Holy Land with good intentions, determined and energetic to do something positive with what we learned. Our peace coalition continues to meet monthly for the first while after our journey. I am excited by the possibilities and have high hopes for our coalition. At a breakfast meeting at Shai's, we brainstorm activities and projects we can undertake.

"We can organize tours similar to ours," Noor suggests. "We can focus on high school students in our respective communities."

Everyone nods in agreement.

Shai adds, "Let's invite teachers and facilitators from the Oasis of Peace to come to Edmonton and put on workshops, youth encounters and conferences."

There is no shortage of ideas. I can feel the energy in the room. Shai promises to compile a list and e-mail it to the group.

By the next month's meeting, it becomes clear we are no longer the same group. Each one of us who made the journey has changed. The experience has also changed the larger group dynamic. A few of the women who did not make the journey to Israel and Palestine begin to feel "left out." During the meeting, Judith, a petite lady in her eighties, who never shies from voicing her opinions, expresses her concerns.

"It's different now," she tells us. "I can sense the closeness between those of you who made the journey. I feel excluded."

Then, early in the spring of 2010, six months after the coalition's journey,

Noor announces she will no longer be attending our monthly meetings.

"I want to pursue other interests now," she says with a hint of apology. She is one of the founding members, and I have the sense our coalition will never be the same. Not long after, more women decide to leave the group.

In July 2010, I attend, with some of the remaining members of the coalition, a presentation at the Old Strathcona Community League given by Judy and Larry Haiven, a husband and wife team who once lived in Edmonton. They are members of Independent Jewish Voices Canada and professors at Saint Mary's University in Halifax, and have recently returned from a study tour of Israel and the Occupied Palestinian Territories. They are visiting cities across Canada, sharing their experiences. Their talk and slide show is entitled, "Israel and Palestine: The Rolling Facts on the Ground." Having seen for myself the reality of the Occupation, I am naturally interested in what they have to say.

When I arrive at the community hall, about 30 people are already seated in rows. I sit down and take my notepad and pen out of my bag. The Haivens' tag-team presentation is detailed and very informative, though for me it does not offer anything new. However, I am always grateful, especially when Jewish people raise awareness about Israel's treatment of Palestinians.

I remember that I promised to give my mother a ride somewhere. Just before the question and answer part of the presentation, I tiptoe my way out of the room, hoping the Haivens are not offended. The following day, I call Bayan, one of the Arab sisters in our coalition, who attended the presentation, to ask how things went.

"It got a little heated," she pauses, before going on to explain. "Some of the Jewish women objected to the presenters' use of the term 'apartheid.'

"Judith hated the presentation. I gave her a ride home afterwards and she lectured me all the way, saying things like, 'Those people are idiots. They can't call it apartheid because there are no separate drinking fountains and there are lots of mixed marriages.'"

I almost cannot fault Judith. She did not make the journey and perhaps she has heard only one side of the Israeli-Palestinian "conflict," perhaps she has never visited the Occupied Palestinian Territories and observed what life is really like for Palestinians. What is disconcerting is to learn that a couple of the Jewish sisters, highly educated and intelligent women who travelled to Palestine and Israel and witnessed for themselves, were upset with the Haivens' comparison of Israel's treatment of Palestinians as being a form of apartheid.

I grab the dictionary on my desk after the call, wanting to confirm my understanding of the word, out of habit. The *Oxford Dictionary of Current English* defines "apartheid," a noun, as "the official system of segregation or discrimination on racial grounds formerly in force in South Africa." While dissimilar to the conflict in South Africa, what I saw not only fits this definition, it is actually much worse.

I feel the walls of my office closing in and decide to take a break, walk around the legislature grounds a block away from work, needing to absorb what I just heard. I know some of the Jewish sisters "got it" well before the journey. I had assumed (humbly) those who did not "get it" would trust what their eyes witnessed, what their ears heard and eventually acknowledge the reality and the reason for the lack of peace in Palestine. It is disappointing for me. Here we are still debating largely man-made terminology, after a decade of dialoguing, after seeing the reality for ourselves. I wonder how these Jewish sisters can reconcile Israel's practice. What word would they be satisfied with that speaks to the Occupation, land confiscations, the demolition of Palestinian homes and the destruction of the environment to build Jewish-only settlements and bypass roads, the network of checkpoints, walls and watchtowers? If a peace coalition of about 20 Jewish and Arab women in Edmonton, thousands of miles removed, cannot agree on the fundamentals, which prevent peace in the Holy Land, then how can we even hope that one day the Arabs and Jews in the Holy Land, and beyond its borders for that matter, will be able to come to some type of viable agreement and achieve peace?

"Seeing is believing," I always trusted.

A few days after the Haivens' presentation, Bayan sends an e-mail to me and the other members of the coalition.

In it she writes:

> I will attend the meeting in September just to let everyone know that it will be my last meeting and why. If, at this late stage in the "conflict," we as a peace and dialogue group cannot agree that the occupation IS the problem, then the group is worthless to me personally and I am moving on to find some other vehicle that will match my passion for sweet justice and love of humanity. There are lots of other groups out there full of passionate, smart, hip people who 'get it.' I am somewhat sorry (not completely because I believe we DO learn things through every experience) that I have allowed myself to be lulled into a semi-conscious state of numb non-articulation for so long about what I have always known to be right and true: the Palestinians exist, they have been completely mistreated and downtrodden by the State of Israel since 1948 and they deserve the same freedom and justice that EVERY living, sentient being does. Period.

I stare in silence at my computer screen. Her words express how I feel. In this moment, I, too, realize it is time for me to dig deeper, do something and divert my energy elsewhere.

Who could have predicted our journey of peace to the Holy Land would also contribute to tearing our coalition into pieces? It has taken less than a year for the Arab Jewish Women's Peace Coalition to dissolve into the ether and become a footnote in our lives. Perhaps this is fate and meant to unfold as it has. Perhaps I am too idealistic or simply naïve for thinking our little coalition could help change things somehow.

Now what? I have all this energy and pent-up passion for peace. Where do I invest it?

There is no formal declaration that the group has disbanded. September's meeting does not materialize and we do not discuss the matter further as a group. I do not know how others feel, but I get together with two of the Jewish women, who are like sisters to me.

I meet Shai at the farmer's market. We stroll from stall to stall, sampling some of the goodies for sale. Eventually, our conversation turns to our coalition.

"How do you feel about our break-up?" I ask.

"The group is just on a 'hiatus,'" she replies, smiling. I sense that she really believes this. I do not respond further and the subject is dropped. I allow myself in the moment to feed the faint glimmer of hope I still harbour.

And, one day over sushi, Hannah, in her calm, matter-of-fact tone, tells me, "It is natural. Everything dies."

She dips her tempura into the small plate of soy sauce and wasabi.

"Our group just died," she says.

"It's disappointing," is all that I can muster as I absentmindedly poke at my food with chopsticks.

It is true our peace coalition is done, but in my heart I know the friendships will endure. I am grateful for my fate, believing my membership with the Arab-Jewish Women's Peace Coalition was my visa into Israel and Palestine. I might not have ventured there on my own. I might still be dreaming to visit.

I will, God willing, return. I just do not know when.

At the end of summer in 2010, the urge to return to the Holy Land creeps in. I feel compelled to show solidarity with the Palestinians, to help, do something tangible, volunteer in some capacity. Early one morning, while searching on the World Wide Web, I discover various ways to do just that. A Google search yields an opportunity with the Alternative Tourism Group, a Joint Advocacy Initiative of the East Jerusalem YMCA/YWCA.

I think about it for a few hours and that afternoon, after satisfying myself the organization was legitimate, I sign up on-line to pick olives in the Bethlehem area for Palestinian farmers during the annual harvest, not because there is a labour shortage, but because they are often harassed, beaten and prevented from accessing their land by Israeli soldiers and settlers. An international presence acts essentially as a human shield.

I break the news to my son during dinner. He puts his fork down and looks up at me from his plate of lasagne.

"Isn't it dangerous to be doing that, Mom?"

"I'll be fine," I try to reassure him. "I am not the only one. People from all around the world have volunteered to help the Palestinians during the olive harvest."

"And that makes it safer?"

He shakes his head and continues eating in silence.

Of course, I am scared! But, I am more tired of doing nothing, of feeling helpless, of throwing my fuzzy slippers at the television screen in frustration when I watch the news and hear the same biased language and misinformation about the Middle East by mainstream media.

A year after the now defunct peace coalition's journey, I am on my way back to the Holy Land. As our plane waits its turn on the runway at Toronto's Pearson airport for a direct flight to Tel Aviv, I re-read an e-mail containing testimonies and tips by previous olive pickers for getting through immigration at Ben Gurion airport in Israel. One seasoned olive picker wrote:

> Make no comments or use words or phrases like 'Palestine,' or 'solidarity,' etc., etc. We are all 'plain dumb tourists' and believe me I've sailed through on all occasions. If held up by immigration for whatever reason, you should have the directions either memorized or printed in your bag. Remain calm, diplomatic though firm as they will let you through even after several hours' wait.

About five minutes after takeoff, I glance out the window and notice that the plane is no longer ascending as it should. The pilot soon confirms my suspicions by announcing that there is some malfunction with the wing light, meaning we have to return to Toronto for an emergency landing, but not before circling the city for several hours trying to burn off fuel.

Palestinian vendors eke out a living selling fruit at a checkpoint near Bethlehem

Israeli-built wall surrounding the Gaza Strip

A Palestinian home cut off from the rest of the community by the Israeli-built wall

Israeli-built wall in Bethlehem

Hebron, Occupied Palestinian Territories

Shuhada Street in the heart of Hebron, now a ghost town

Line-up at dawn, Qalandia Checkpoint in the Occupied Palestinian Territories

Palestinians wait for Israeli soldiers to open the "Humanitarian Gate" at Qalandia Checkpoint

Elderly Palestinian tries to cross Qalandia Checkpoint

International volunteers pick olives near Bethlehem

Author picks olives near Beit Jala in the Occupied Palestinian Territories

A peace sign made by volunteer olive pickers

One entrance to Aida Refugee Camp; the key represents keys to homes that once belonged to Palestinians but were confiscated or destroyed

Installed by Palestinians, a protective mesh covers a street in Hebron to catch debris thrown down by settlers

Israeli soldiers stop international olive pickers and local farmers to check IDs

Author interviews Palestinian teenager living near Bethlehem

Israeli soldiers fire tear gas and sound bombs at demonstrators in Bil'n in Occupied Palestinian Territories

Palestinian men photograph demonstrators in Bil'n

Palestinian looks out at nearby settlements encircling her village near Bethlehem

Israeli-built Wall, Bethlehem

Israeli-built Wall and Watchtower, Aida Refugee Camp

Part Two

TEN

Forced Evictions in the Jerusalem Neighbourhood of Sheikh Jarrah

My dilemma was to live quietly and obediently in a country that helped make me into a refugee and that I chose to make my home, pretending it is the greatest home for justice in the world. Or I could go back to Palestine and live miserably under Israeli occupation and possibly die fighting injustice. I chose the lesser of the two evils. But I was boiling inside to find out that convincing even one American of the truth of what had happened to my people and my homeland was quickly and continuously negated by press coverage portraying my victimized brothers as terrorists. At the same time, the U.S. press described the killers of my brothers and sisters as heroic people fighting for security with American weapons paid for by tax dollars to which I contributed.

Aziz Shihab, Does the Land Remember Me?
A Memoir of Palestine, *2007*

It is Saturday morning, October 16, 2010. I have made it back to the "sacred" city. Jerusalem.

"We have to head south on Nablus Road," I say to Martha after checking my map. She is a quiet, white-haired activist from England that I met at breakfast. It turned out we are staying at the same hotel and volunteering for the same olive harvest campaign in the Bethlehem area. We have the whole day to ourselves and decided to start with the Old City of Jerusalem.

"That way," I point to the right.

I should be exhausted. Instead, I feel energized. After my aborted flight in Toronto, EL AL officials promptly provided a new airplane and crew, two hours following a safe touchdown, and I still arrived in time yesterday to have dinner as planned that evening with nine of the international volunteer olive pickers.

We walk three blocks to the end of Nablus Road, cross Sultan Sulaiman Street and descend a series of wide, stone steps leading to Damascus Gate. I notice Martha's cheeks, already reddened by the sun. Before we reach the peaked archway of stone set in the ancient wall surrounding the Old City, I stop. Martha waits beside me while I take one last look at my map before folding it up. Typically, I need to know where I am, what I am looking at and constantly carry a map of the place I am travelling in. Today I feel like getting lost. Not that you actually can in the Old City; it just seems that way in parts where the street's trajectory is concealed from view. Besides, I have visited the Old City before and have some idea of its layout.

"How about we let the wind take us where it wants," I say to Martha, slipping the map into my bag.

"That would be wonderful."

She nods her head enthusiastically.

I stare up at the peaked stone arch as we cross the threshold, and follow the L-shaped, entranceway, built that way strategically to slow invading marauders. We stroll through a market along a cobblestone street that slopes down, accommodated with a series of implanted stone steps at various intervals. As they have for generations, Palestinian women dressed in traditional embroidered dresses sit patiently on the steps, beside plastic crates filled with bunches of fresh parsley and mint, and piles of lettuce and onions, many of which have been likely harvested from small, back-yard gardens and brought here to sell. One of them is talking on her mobile phone. Once I am a few metres away, I turn around and take her photograph, amused by the merging of modernity and antiquity.

Martha and I follow Al-Wad Street, running generally north-south through the Muslim Quarter, passing shops selling t-shirts with political messages and an antique shop with a dusty, green sign inviting shoppers inside:

COME IN. STEP BACK IN TIME 2000 YEARS

In many ways it does feel like stepping back in time, dreamlike to be walking literally where prophets once walked, a blessing to tread over the stone surface of the streets, shiny and smoothed over millennia. My eyes roam the small shops on both sides of the street, selling a variety of things: fast food and fresh fruit and vegetables, handbags and belly dancing outfits.

"I smell frankincense," I say to Martha and follow my nose to a cubby-hole shop where a vendor is burning some over hot charcoal in a brass brazier. The heavenly smell takes me back to my childhood. On a small table, terracotta bowls brim with different types of frankincense: black, yellow, white and orange. I had not known that there were so many kinds. I pick up one of the rock-like pieces and admire it. Frankincense has been used for more than 5,000 years for its healing properties, one of the gifts for Jesus brought by the three wise men, according to the Bible.

"My mother used to burn frankincense when we were sick and to ward off the evil eye," I say to the middle-aged vendor. "Give me two handfuls. A mixture, please."

He smiles, "As you wish, Madam."

He fills a small bag, taking a pinch from each bowl and weighs it.

"Twenty shekels," he says, and starts to fill another bag.

"That will be enough for now, thank you," I tell him.

"It's a gift from me," he says.

"*Shukrun.* That's very generous of you, but it's not necessary."

I place my hand on my chest, shaking my head, hoping not to offend him.

"For your mother," he insists. I cave in and take the two small bags from his outstretched hand.

Further on, we pass a spice shop. Tables are covered with piles of oregano, cumin, curry and other spices shaped into mini pyramids. Another spice vendor close by has his wares in plastic bins with white labels in Arabic and English: cinnamon, sumac, nutmeg and saffron.

The Muslim Quarter bustles with local Arabs and Jews, tourists and pilgrims. But there are also omnipresent squads of Israeli soldiers and police. Out of place in this sacred city, their presence ruins the natural ambience and reminds me of the cruel reality of the present, but I do not allow myself to dwell on them. An invisible energy emanates from the Old City — its spirit is much stronger. My senses are heightened and overshadow such thoughts as I take in the plethora of colours and the fusion of smells that fill the air: freshly baked pastries, cardamom-flavoured coffee and fried falafel. I tune in to the mingling of sounds: shoppers haggling over prices, sellers yelling out their wares, "Two eggplant for one shekel. Two eggplant." And, from a speaker at the back of one shop, Fairuz, a much-loved and famous Lebanese, singing, *Ya dara doori fina.*

Vendors call out to me as I pass by.

"Madam, pashmina scarf?"

"*La. Shukrun.*"

"Madam, silver jewellery?"

"*La. Shukrun.*"

I am not in the mood to shop. For now, I just want to look. There is so much to see. My eyes do not know where to look, or at times what they are looking at.

A woman sits on newspaper with her back against a wall of a tunnel-like street. In the dimness, I almost trip over her. Teetering on one leg, I manage to see her and stop at the last second. I glance down and apologize. She is completely covered in black, even her face and hands. Her head is bent down. A red prayer rug is draped over her crossed legs. She does not look up and appears to be waiting for a compassionate soul to drop some loose change into her lap, but I do not notice any money in it. I assume from the small frame that she is a *she*, but I cannot say with certainty. Perhaps she is not begging; I do not know for sure. As I walk away, I look back over my shoulder at her, mindful of how lucky I am for winning the "birth lottery." It is bittersweet.

We reach a section of the Via Dolorosa, where we come across a small group of pilgrims carrying a large, wooden cross, stopped at one of the Stations of the Cross. I watch them for a few minutes, their heads bowed in prayer. It dawns on me that I know very little about this Christian tradition. "It would be a unique experience to witness this ritual at Easter," I think to myself.

We carry on and come to a small church. I stop to take photographs. A sign above the arched doorway reads:

BIRTHPLACE OF THE VIRGIN MARY.

"Really? How do they know that?" I wonder to myself, wanting this to be true. The Virgin Mary is revered by Muslims, too. An entire chapter in the Holy Qur'an is dedicated to her. I have always had an inexplicable affinity for different places of prayer, regardless of the religion practiced within them. I remember one Sunday as a 13-year-old. Out of curiosity, I accompanied my Catholic friend to church without telling my parents. Not out of fear of being punished; I did not know how they would have reacted. Rather, I did not know what I would say to explain the *why* behind my action when I barely appreciated it for myself. I was searching without knowing I was searching.

Martha and I end up at the Western Wall, Judaism's holiest site. We walk across a large courtyard to the women's side of the open air synagogue. I find an empty spot along the base of the ancient wall and pray, for peace. I remember my *kvitlach*, Hebrew word for prayer or message. I pull out the folded piece of paper from my pocket, on which I had written one of my favourite verses from the Qur'an: *O humanity. We created you from a male and female and created you into tribes so that you may come to know one another.*

I stuff the *kvitlach* in one of the cracks between the huge stones of the wall, along with the hundreds of other prayers that have been left here.

—⁊—

Later in the day, Martha and I join Paulo and several other peace activists from England on a 10-minute walk from our hotel to the Palestinian neighbourhood of Sheikh Jarrah in occupied East Jerusalem. About 3,000

Palestinians live there. Our plan is to visit some of the families Israel evicted from their homes, then handed those homes over to Jewish settlers. As we follow Paulo north of the Old City along Nablus Road, I remember reading that it was once a major access corridor. Israeli authorities closed a stretch of this road after 74 Jewish people, mostly doctors and nurses, were killed on their way to Hadassah Hospital by Arab forces during the 1948 Arab-Israeli war. It seems every corner of Jerusalem has a tragic story. It seems, too, that Israel covets every corner of Jerusalem. Sheikh Jarrah's location within the "Holy Basin," has become a curse, as I will discover.

"We are almost there," Paulo says, looking back at me before turning right on Othman Ibn Affan Street. As we stroll along, I think about the story behind the naming of Sheikh Jarrah, which I had read up on before coming here. It was named after Husam al-Din al-Jarrahi, reportedly, Saladin's doctor. Al-Jarrahi's tomb dates back to 1201 and lies inside a mosque off Nablus Road. The romantic in me wonders if the family I married into is related to the doctor.

Rifqa Al-Kurd and her daughter, Maysa, are standing on the street in front of their yard. Paulo approaches them and they shake hands. He has been here before and their smiles become even wider upon recognizing him. We introduce ourselves. They are friendly and accustomed to hosting international activists, including Israeli peace activists, even famous activists like former President Jimmy Carter, who visit to show their support.

We turn our attention to a two-story building across the street from Rifqa's yard. A gigantic candelabrum sits on the roof and Israeli flags are strung across the second-floor façade. We stand there for a while, watching a man at ground level, I assume a reporter, pointing a video camera through the bars of the front gate at a Jewish settler, who faces him squarely as if in a standoff. I photograph the scene.

"That building belongs to the Hanoun and al-Ghawe families," Rifqa tells me. "Settlers occupied it on August 9, 2009, with the help of Israeli soldiers and police. They have no conscience, no mercy. In a matter of an hour, they left 58 people homeless, 20 of them children."

My eyes follow her slender finger as she points further down the street.

"Some members of the Hanoun family pitched a tent under that fig tree beside the road," she says. "They refused to leave. They lived on the street in front of their house for over five months."

The atmosphere is tense. Violence seethes in the background, on some invisible cusp, ready to erupt at any moment. It is unnerving to know that in the past Israeli soldiers and police have beaten and arrested international activists for protesting peacefully on this same street where we are standing in front of the Al-Kurd yard. This street has witnessed bloodshed and families become homeless. It is quiet now, but it was not like this yesterday, when locals, Israeli and international activists from around the world congregated on this same street to protest the illegal evictions in Sheikh Jarrah.

Rifqa steers us inside her rectangular-shaped yard. She is nearly 90 years old, slightly-built, yet she carries herself upright, radiating strength, resilience and defiance. Her dress appears to be handmade and the scarf tied under her chin covers her hair, framing a translucent complexion blotched with sun spots. She reminds me of a stereotypical Ukrainian grandmother. We follow her along a wide, stone sidewalk.

"That's my son's house, Nabil," Rifqa says, pointing to a small stone house fronted by an abandoned garden strewn with two couch cushions, a headless doll and plastic bags.

"He built it more than 10 years ago when my twin grandsons were born and our house became too crowded. Israel rejected our application for a permit to build. We built anyway. We were taken to court and lost. The judge himself locked the house. It stayed locked up and empty for years before my son finally moved his family into it. Not long after, on November 3, 2009, settlers took my son's home. They threw his belongings outside and occupied it. His family has been living with me since."

"There are three settlers inside right now," she tells us as we take a seat inside the sit-in or solidarity tent beside Nabil's house. This is where local and international activists often congregate and conduct sit-ins to show their support for Palestinians and their opposition to the confiscation and occupation of Palestinian homes and lands in Sheikh Jarrah. Rifqa lives in an older, smaller home behind her son's house, which she and her late husband built in 1956.

Maysa brings out a thermos of Arabic coffee and pours us each a small cup. Then she disappears and comes back carrying two posters of photographs, a visual essay showing scenes of settler and Palestinian confrontations and violence by Israeli soldiers against demonstrators last summer after two, large Palestinian families were evicted from their homes.

She holds the posters up, allowing time for us to gaze at the collection of photographs. One captures her brother standing in the garden. Around him, the yard is littered with his household belongings. Next to this is a photograph of soldiers hauling away a demonstrator, a woman, whose face is painted in multiple colours like a clown.

"Come, I want to show you how we live," Rifqa says, getting up. "There's barely any room for all of us."

Some of us follow her into her modest two-room house.

"It is not enough they took my son's house and stuck themselves in our faces every day, they plan also to take my house," she says as she leads us through the rooms. "Twelve of us are now crammed in here."

It is clean, but cluttered; boxes are stacked high in the corners along with smaller pieces of furniture, kitchen items and a child's bicycle.

"I have to appear in court in January of next year to face an eviction notice."

"God forbid. If you are evicted, where will you go?" I think out loud.

"Where can we go? What choices do we have?" she replies tiredly. "*Alhamdulillah.*"

I admire her faith. After everything she has endured, she still thanks God.

While we were inside, a female reporter and cameraman have shown up, as if visits by reporters were a normal activity. Just yesterday, in front of Rifqa's house, settlers clashed with demonstrators and local residents of Sheikh Jarrah. Police responded with tear gas and beat a small boy. I assume that is why they are here. The man tightens his camera to a tripod. Maysa sits on a couch outside the door of her mother's house, smoothes her *hijab*, appearing calm and comfortable in front of the camera pointed at her. The reporter also wants to interview Rifqa. As she waits her turn, we chat on a tiled patio between the two homes.

"Where did you live before Sheikh Jarrah?" I ask her.

"I'm originally from Haifa. Like many we fled here in 1948. The Jordanian government and the UN gave us this plot and allowed us to build our house in exchange for relinquishing our refugee status. I was widowed early and had to raise two children on my own."

It hurts to hear that she was a refugee once and now, more than 60 years later, she lives in constant danger of being dispossessed and displaced once again.

"I have little hope. Israel intends to take over Sheikh Jarrah," she says after a brief moment of silence. "The law is on the side of the settlers and soldiers, but we will not leave. No, we will sleep on the streets or in our cars if we have to."

Maysa finishes her interview and seems energized. There is quickness in her stride as she walks several metres across the patio to her brother's confiscated house. She peers through the window and motions for me to come and look. Her boldness rubs off on me. Without thinking, I approach the window and take a quick peek inside. One man is sprawled out on a couch, a newspaper hides his face, and the other two are sitting at a table watching a small television.

"They beat us and when we complain to the police. They say we beat them and we are the ones to get arrested," Maysa explains. "They throw their garbage at us and play loud music. They call me 'Miss Piggy.'"

She has a hurt look. I assume the settlers meant to ridicule her stout build.

"Aren't you afraid of them?" I ask.

"They are the cowards," her voice rises in exasperation. "They are more afraid. They know what they are doing to us is wrong."

The men inside must know we are at the window. I am certain they can hear Maysa, but they ignore us.

"Let's join the others," I say, making my way to the sit-in area. She follows, chuckling at the nervous quiver in my voice.

A middle-aged man of medium build steps into the yard. I am guessing he is a neighbour or relative of Rifqa. He is eager, like most Palestinians I meet, to talk about their displacement and what they continue to endure. When I introduce myself and he realizes I speak Arabic, he says, "My English is not that good. Would you please translate to the group for me?"

I nod in agreement. "*Ma fe mishkali.* That's not a problem."

"Come with me," he says. We follow him to the street in front of Rifqa's yard where he stops.

"I live over there," he points to a cluster of houses spilling down the hillside to the north of us, and lists off the names of some of the foreign embassies perched on the slope: Belgium, Spain, Italy and Turkey.

"Sheikh Jarrah is an important neighbourhood. Israel has been confiscating parts of it since 1967," he explains. "It took an olive grove on a hill to the east known as Karm al-Mufti and other sites in the area to build Jewish settlements.

"Life here is very stressful. I cannot work. I am forced to rely on my son and daughter's work to bring in money for the family. My house has an eviction order against it, too. I will be going to court next month."

He stops and we file behind him back to the sit-in area.

"Settlers throw garbage at us," he continues after we sit down. "They break our windows and paint hateful graffiti on our homes and fences. They swear at us and say, 'Mohamed is a pig.' They play loud music. They beat small children and old men and women. Their government pays them to occupy Palestinian homes. Israel is taking more and more families to court.

"Israel does not want peace. It wants a Jewish-only Jerusalem. It is forcing us out to prevent a Palestinian capital in Jerusalem. It has the power. I have little hope. It's like going through a war. My children are traumatized. They have nightmares and wet their beds. They sleepwalk. My children's school grades dropped from the 90s to the 40s. They have no future here. We have no alternatives. Where are we going to go? But we will not give up."

Paulo, who is sitting to my right, turns to me.

"I have a question for him. Can you translate for me?"

"Certainly."

I notice Abou Alaa lean forward in his chair in anticipation.

"Ask Abou Alaa, 'How can we help?'"

"We want to be treated like human beings," Abou Alaa replies straight away in a pained voice, looking squarely at Paulo, who tears up when I translate.

"Put pressure on your governments," he continues, looking around at us, "Tell people in your countries about our situation, how we live."

At that, Abou Alaa stands up. He shakes our hands, thanks us for listening to him and leaves. By now it is late afternoon. I am aware suddenly that time had raced imperceptibly during the few hours we spent here.

"We have to catch our bus to Bethlehem," Paulo tells us, and we prepare to leave.

"Come back and visit us," Rifqa says, kissing me three times on the cheek. "Tell the people in Canada what you saw with your own eyes."

"*Insha'Allah*," I reply, not knowing I will hear that same simple request over and over during my stay in the Occupied Palestinian Territories.

"I'll do my best," I look her in the eye. "I will come visit you after the olive harvest. I promise. I have time before returning home."

"*Ma'alsalaama*, go in peace, *habibti*."

She hugs me.

"*Ma'alsalaama*."

I wave goodbye.

ELEVEN

Biblical Beit Sahour

The olive picking campaign made me stronger, more independent and I don't complain anymore. I saw the strength of the Palestinians and they gave me some of their strength and power. I now have more knowledge about the conflict and can make people more aware. And, of course, keep hope alive in my lifetime!

Sabah Fizazzi, Peace activist and olive picker volunteer
from the Netherlands, October 2011, e-mail

We are a few minutes late when we arrive at the Alternative Tourism Group (ATG) office, where the seventh annual 2010 olive harvest campaign is being hosted. ATG is a Palestinian NGO based out of Beit Sahour, a predominately Christian Palestinian village located less than two kilometres east of Bethlehem. The meeting room, seemingly emptied of furniture, is crowded with about 50 people. Some are sitting on the floor while others are standing. A few glance up as the six of us pause near the doorway. They shuffle closer together making room for us on the tiled floor.

"Welcome," a young man in his twenties says, lifting his hand to wave us in. "Please join us. Find a spot to sit. I am Baha."

He has long, curly hair tucked inside a black knitted beanie. He looks relaxed speaking in front of a group and has already started the briefing for the olive picking program.

"The heat wave caused by global warming has affected the olive yield," he explains. "In better years, Palestinians in the Bethlehem area harvest about

35,000 tons of olives, annually. This year they expect to harvest only 11,000 tons. Many olive fields were also destroyed when Israel took parts of this biblical village to build the Har Homa settlement, a concrete segregation wall and several checkpoints along its northern edge.

"Daily attacks from settlers and soldiers are common everywhere in the West Bank, especially now, during the olive harvest. Each field has a story, a history. Last week, settlers burned one farmer's entire olive grove. In yet another field, settlers stole the olives as soon as the farmer finished picking them. In a different field, Israeli soldiers watched as settlers beat the farmer and his family when they tried to pick their own olives."

Baha tells us that we can expect a confrontation with soldiers and settlers. I glance around. The room is packed with peace activists of various ages and ethnicities. There are many smiles. No one seems surprised or concerned. Instead, anticipation and excitement fill the air. I feel blessed to be part of a group of volunteers from around the world, who came here with a shared purpose and seemingly a common base of understanding about the reality in the Occupied Palestinian Territories. I am excited to meet them all and hear their stories. I thank God silently for the privilege of being here to learn and help in some small yet meaningful way.

"Tomorrow, we will be helping a farmer in Beit Jala," Baha continues. "If soldiers show up tomorrow, or after tomorrow, let the farmers do the talking. You're not here to be confrontational. Israeli soldiers and settlers are capable of shooting you or deporting you. You're here to learn and to show solidarity with the Palestinians."

"May I take photographs?" I ask.

"You can take photographs," he pauses, "until you are told to stop. A filmmaker and his crew will be joining us to document the olive harvest. Feel free to give them an interview if they ask you for one."

As he smiles, his permanent dimples deepen.

"But, if a soldier asks you for your name, give them a false one."

Laughter erupts.

"That is it for the briefing," he tells us. "Relax while we call your host families so they can pick you up."

I chose to make the most of this experience by staying with a local Palestinian family. Another group of 50 volunteers opted to stay at the Sahara Hotel in Beit Sahour. I socialize with the other volunteers as I wait for my host family to arrive. Among our group are six women from Korea, ranging in ages, 10 people from the Netherlands (three of them young students of Moroccan descent), couples from Spain, France, New Zealand, England and the United States. There are two of us from Canada, myself and a lady from Toronto.

It turns out that I am paired up with Martha from England. We will be staying with a Christian Palestinian family. We step outside to wait with the other volunteers. It is past nine in the evening when a young man pulls up in front of the ATG office. He exits his car and approaches us. We are the only ones left.

"Martha and Carmen?" he asks.

"I'm Carmen," I say, shaking his hand.

"I'm Martha, pleasure to meet you."

"My name is Ra'id. Sorry to keep you waiting."

He helps us load our bags in the trunk. I sit in the back with Martha. The five-minute ride to his house is quiet. His mother, who lives on the main floor of the three-story stone building, is not at home when we arrive. Ra'id points out the bathrooms and shows us to our rooms. Sleep arrives quickly.

I wake up at dawn, in the same position I fell asleep in, and it takes a few seconds for the mental fog to lift and to realize where I am. The house is still. I dress and head outside to explore before breakfast. I follow a sloping street south, enjoying the quietness. To the east, the sky above the sleepy hills of Beit Sahour is lit up in hues of lavender and pink. To the north, on a higher ridge overlooking the village, sits a Jewish settlement. I read these hills were once a pine forest. The highest summits have now been razed and replaced with the rows of densely-built, white stone apartments and condos. The settlement stands out, sterile and eerie in the morning light, alien on the biblical landscape, a fortress choking the hilltop.

I continue walking. It is surreal being in Beit Sahour.

"Beit Sahour," I say out loud, slightly amused, aware how easily the words roll off my tongue. Its Arabic name means, "house of those who stay up late." It is here in this biblical village, nicknamed Shepherd's Field, where some say angels appeared to shepherds and gave news of Jesus's birth.

How many people can say they spent two weeks sleeping next to Shepherd's Field?

I am hoping to stumble across one of the two sites where this event is said to have occurred. But, I forgot to bring my map, so I do not venture far. I head back after a few blocks, slowly, wanting the energy of the place to permeate me.

At eight in the morning, the olive pickers congregate on the narrow sloped street in front of the ATG office. Bells chime at the Lutheran Church across the street. I feel the excitement as we all pitch in to load ladders, tarps, buckets and cases of bottled water into the belly of the bus.

From Beit Sahour, our bus heads northwest towards the Palestinian village of Beit Jala. We go through Bethlehem and cross the checkpoint without a long wait. About 10 minutes later, the bus stops on a plateau along the side of Highway 60. The concrete monster wall runs parallel to the road, connecting Har Homa settlement to the west with Gilo settlement to the east. Rows of stone terraces follow the contours of the land down the *wadi*, where we will be picking. The spot is familiar. I took a photograph of this olive grove from the window of our bus as we were heading south for a tour of Hebron in 2009. I had no way of knowing then that exactly one year later, I would be picking olives on the same slope. I have to remind myself that this is not a dream.

Tarik, the Palestinian landowner, meets us on the side of the highway. I sense eyes on us and assume Israeli soldiers in the nearby watchtower are watching as we unload the items stored in the bus and follow Tarik, in a single file, along the dusty footpath down the terraced slopes to the *wadi* bottom, before dipping out of the soldiers' field of sight.

There, we crowd around Tarik for a quick lesson in olive picking. His three young children and his brother are also here. Tarik places a blue tarp under one of the olive trees like a Christmas tree skirt and demonstrates how to hold the branch in one hand and run our fingers over it with the other, pulling the olives off in one fluid motion and letting them fall on the tarp below.

We set to work. Some begin to place tarps under the trees. Others stand on ladders and pick olives. Some climb up the olive trees to get to the higher branches, while others pick the fallen olives from the tarps and put them into buckets and then bags capable of carrying about 50 kilograms. I climb up one of the ladders to pick. The film of dust covering the olive trees soon causes me to begin sneezing. The ladder bobbles. I step down and join Catherine, a pleasant lady from the United States who is a return volunteer. I sit next to her on the ground in the shade of a tree. She rummages in her bag and pulls out a pill box.

"Here, an antihistamine will help," she says, handing it to me. "I think I'm allergic to olives. I'm having problems breathing and am running a temperature." Her white complexion is flushed pink and glints with beads of sweat.

As I wait for my bouts of sneezing to end and the antihistamine to kick in, I watch the Korean women. They work hard, undeterred by the blazing sun, and do not move to a new tree until every olive is picked. I admire their work ethic and decide to join them. I want to know what made them volunteer to pick olives in the Holy Land. As we work, I start a conversation with the youngest of the ladies, a bubbly beauty named Solby, who speaks English and translates for some of the other Korean women.

"We belong to a group called Imagine Peace," she tells me from her perch in the tree.

I am interested in learning more, but before we finish our conversation, I hear a vehicle. I stop picking and look up the slope to my left in the direction of the sound. An Israeli military jeep drives by on a narrow road higher up. I watch as it disappears around a bend, leaving a curly cloud of dust behind. I am aware how even a momentary glimpse of the army's presence brought everything to a halt and made my heart race.

The trees are not full at the *wadi* bottom and are even sparser as we ascend the terraced hillside belonging to Tarik's family, unlike the bountiful olive groves I have seen in the more rural areas.

During a brief conversation, Tarik tells me, "I own 132 olive trees, but I can't tend to them. They used to produce over 700 kilograms. Now, I am expecting to harvest only about 300 kilograms.

"I was beaten twice by settlers. Earlier this year, they set fire to my vineyard."

At noon, we zigzag our way further up the slope, over north-south stone terraces dotted with more olive trees, to Tarik's ancestral home. His family lives in Bethlehem. The small stone hut hugging the side of the slope functions as a summer cabin, which they use to watch over their olive grove. I take a spot at the back of the string of olive pickers, who are standing at the end of a long table set on a stone courtyard. Tarik's mother, a lively woman, is dishing out *maqlouba*, a traditional Palestinian dish. I introduce myself as she piles some on my plate.

"*Ahlan habibti*," she beams. "It's a pleasure meeting you. I look forward to talking with you later."

She hands me a container of yoghurt and, not meaning to be rude, turns her attention to the next person in line.

"This land has been owned by my family for generations," Tarik tells us after we finish eating. "I have a land deed dating back to Ottoman times."

As I listen to Tarik, I think how proof of ownership seems to matter little in the Occupied Palestinian Territories.

"After the Oslo Peace Accords, Israel confiscated more than half my land," he says, pointing to the Wall on the opposite slopes and the roads on either side of it. "They are built on my land. Israel uprooted the olive trees that once grew there, some of them fifty and sixty years old."

Tarik stops when he notices his mother carrying a large pot in each hand. He walks over, takes them from her and sets them down as she heads back inside.

"Please, help yourself to sage tea and coffee," he tells us. "But, before you start, I want to thank every one of you. It makes me happy that you cared enough to come here and help me harvest my olive grove."

I pour myself a small cup of tea and take a seat. Tarik's mother joins me, after looking around at our group to make sure everyone has helped themselves.

"I can tell by your accent that you're Lebanese," she smiles warmly and pats my knee. "Where did you learn to speak Arabic in Canada?"

"My father insisted we speak Arabic at home while we were growing up." Not meaning to boast, I add that later, as an adult, I taught myself how to read the language.

"Bravo!"

Her big brown eyes sparkle with enthusiasm and she leans over, hugging me like a proud mother.

Later, one by one, the olive pickers thank her for lunch, shake her hand and smile in appreciation.

"Come back and visit," she tells me as we say goodbye. "Take my telephone number."

I hand her my notebook and pen and she writes it down.

"You'll always be welcomed in our home at any time."

"*Shukrun* for everything," I say. "It was a pleasure to meet you."

I am amazed by how quickly I have become attached to her.

We carry the ladders, buckets and other belongings and walk south about half a kilometre towards the highway, where our bus is parked. I glance back at the dusty time-worn hills and terraces of stubborn olive trees clinging to the thirsty earth. I am covered in red dust and delighted to have helped, albeit in a small way. There is no labour shortage in the Occupied Palestinian Territories. The olive harvest is an annual activity for Palestinian farmers. So too in more recent years, is the Alternative Tourism Group's recruitment of international volunteers. Organizers of the olive harvest campaign hope that our presence will act as a deterrent against violence — that settlers and soldiers will think twice. Our presence is a gesture that says we stand in solidarity with Palestinians living under Israel's military occupation — that we hear and see their suffering.

TWELVE

Bethlehem:
Some Walls Can Speak

You cannot measure the psychological impact of the wall. You
can't capture it in words or images. Nor can you control it or be
treated for it or push it away. This ghost never goes away, and
it always controls your consciousness, even when you sleep, the
nightmare grabs hold of you.

Mundher Elias al-Bandak, "Living in the Shadow of the Wall"
(Bethlehem District) Ida Audeh, The Electronic Intifada
November 16, 2003

Some walls can speak. In the Bethlehem district there is an eight-metre-
high, 15-kilometre-long Israeli-built "separation wall" screaming to be
heard.

From the village of Beit Jala, where we spent the morning picking
olives, we head north a couple of kilometres for a tour of the Wall where it
cuts through the city of Bethlehem and runs along its north-west limits. A
middle-aged man meets us on the side of a road near the northern outskirts
of Bethlehem, where we are stopped.

"Welcome," he says with a smile. He waits for us all to pile out of the bus
and quiet down before continuing. "My name is Yusuf. I will be your guide
today.

"You can't see it, but over there is Rachel's Tomb and Bilal Ibn Rabah
Mosque," he says, pointing to the bottom of the valley in the distance.

I look past the chain link fence bordering the road, standing on a height of land overlooking what was once a pastoral panorama, a valley of stone terraces and olive trees that has been truncated by a series of walls. One runs in an east-west direction and is intersected by two parallel walls extending north and south.

Yusuf is right. I cannot see any of its structures because the site is hidden from view, literally squared off by walls.

"It's a sacred site for Muslims and Jews. Israel deemed this religious site and bordering olive grove off-limits to Palestinians," he tells us. "Now, only Jewish people can visit the site."

I stare at the side-by-side, massive, rectangular slabs of concrete jutting up from the ground. The Wall slithers over the landscape like a greedy anaconda, swallowing up villages in its path and gobbling up finite aquifers and adjacent fertile land owned by Palestinians — walling in the dead and walling out the living.

I am aware that this is not going to be a typical tour. I doubt that a stroll along the base of the Wall is part of the standard tour itinerary in the Holy Land. Yet, I cannot stop thinking: *How can tourists and pilgrims visiting Bethlehem miss the concrete monstrosity on the landscape?* I wonder what Christian pilgrims in particular think.

How do they feel when they see the network of colossal concrete walls surrounding Christ's birthplace, embedded with watchtowers, checkpoints and military bases?

I am overwhelmed by emotions and a sense of futility every time I see the Wall, sucked into a vortex of sadness and frustration against my will. I don't know if I am more infuriated by the Israelis who built it, the Americans who financed it or world leaders, in particular Arab leaders, who continue to pretend it doesn't exist. It is too painful to think they don't care. I tell myself, "People would care, if they knew." With America's backing, Israel has turned this holy city, where many believe Jesus was born, into a prison for Palestinians.

We board the bus and, a few minutes later, we are dropped off near a checkpoint at the north edge of Bethlehem, where we are confronted with more walls. The retractable metal gate, built in the Wall, is closed. The scene makes me feel as if I am walking towards a maximum security prison.

It is a virtual prison for Palestinians.

Two sections of the Wall converge at right angles. I stare up at the concrete watchtower in the corner, rising well above the Wall, manned with Israeli soldiers who have an unobstructed, 360-degree view of the surrounding hills. Not only does the Wall prevent Palestinians from moving freely to and from the city, limiting their opportunities, it must also seep into their psyche, inhibit their thoughts and aspirations, and emphasize their otherness.

It is difficult to believe my own eyes — to accept. I cannot help feeling as though I have fallen down the rabbit hole. It is a surreal and jumbled dream, where immorality is moral and abnormal is normal. I feel trapped, dwarfed and defenseless against the powers that perpetuate this inhumanity. I am guilt-ridden, too, because I am free and my fellow Arabs are not. Worst of all, I fear my hidden anger might turn into hate. *God forbid.*

Our group walks up to its base, posing for photographs. Colourful murals and political graffiti minimize the inescapable dreariness of the martial-grey Wall and matching watchtower, which someone has painted huge cracks on.

"Would you like me to take your photograph?" Sabah asks me, holding out her hand to take my camera. She is one of the olive pickers from the Netherlands.

"I'd appreciate that. Thank you."

I pass it to her and stand at the base of the Wall, suddenly feeling like an insignificant insect. Out of habit, I view the image Sabah has just captured on my camera, and realize how well I blend into the background. My shirt is the same orange as the row of gargantuan flowers painted along the bottom third of the Wall. The round centers of the flowers are profile silhouettes of people looking at each other. The faces are painted in different colours, from light beige to black, representing the diverse shades of humanity. Towering above the row of flowers is a gigantic pink bow and the caption:

WITH LOVE AND KISSES. NOTHING LASTS FOREVER.

We bypass the checkpoint and walk further south, following the road bordered by a north-south segment of the Wall. As much as I am repulsed by the Wall, I'm also intrigued by the layers of graffiti and artwork left by locals, tourists and international activists. The presence of the Wall is a violent action in and of itself, yet it is being used as an outlet for expression, a method of non-violent resistance that uses rhetorical techniques, humour and meaningful art to express opposition to its existence. The graffiti seems to have cultivated a life and character of its own, continually expanding and evolving. Many have just painted their names or initials and the date they were here. There is unity in the diversity of voices, a profusion of political and emotional outpouring. The bottom half of the Wall here is one, continuous canvas. There is too much to read and too little time, so I take photographs for later, when I can contemplate the satirical murals, and the blatant and not so blatant messages:

TEAR DOWN THIS WALL.

TO EXIST IS TO RESIST.

ONLY GOD CAN JUDGE. NOBODY ELSE.

PLAY AS IF YOU'LL DIE TOMORROW. LEARN AS IF YOU'LL LIVE FOREVER.

Amina, another activist and volunteer of Moroccan descent living in the Netherlands, stops at the end of one of the giant murals along the base of the Wall. With her back to me, she is barely distinguishable and blends into a cartoon painting in which nine life-size silhouettes of children of different ages stand facing a large breach in the wall. Their arms are raised. Some are giving the peace sign or hoisting the Palestinian flag above their heads. Set within the line of children is Handala, the famous cartoon character, a 10-year-old Palestinian refugee, who is always depicted barefoot and with his back to the world. Handala has become a symbol of non-violent resistance against the Occupation. I capture a picture of Amina writing FREE PALESTINE on the Wall. I turn my attention to a 30-metre caption above the strip of artwork and graffiti. Scrawled in baby blue paint is:

YOU STOLE OUR LAND YET WE ARE CALLED THE CRIMINALS.

The caption is signed by: FIRAS T.

I continue walking at the tail end of our group. The road rises. We come to a fork in the road, where we stop. At the summit of the hill sits a solitary three-story house. It has been cordoned off on three sides by the Wall. I gasp in disbelief as I process what I am witnessing, overwhelmed by the senselessness. The house is newer-looking; white stone covers the sides. Water tanks grow from its flat roof and its exterior blinds have been squeezed shut. There are no signs of its inhabitants. Its only open side is fronted by a neglected patch of ground littered with the remnants of what appears to be a demolished home. Clumps of weeds grow between the crumbling sides of an old stone fence. Mounds of garbage spill onto a paved walkway abutting the road. It dawns on me that the people living inside once had a 360-degree view of the picturesque hills and valleys around them. Those living on the first and second floors now have the Wall staring back at them from three sides.

"This is unbearably wrong," I mutter to myself, and contemplate the psychological effect of waking up every morning, opening the blinds and having the Wall for a view, a daily reminder that there is no escaping it, that it controls you, that you are its prisoner. It is difficult for me to imagine living like this. I really do not know what I would do if this was my house, my sanctuary.

What can a mere mortal like me do against such an enormity?

We continue walking east, along another road in Bethlehem. The Wall follows the road before cutting deeper into the city. Here, the graffiti and graphics have become comical. I am surprised and amused to come across a painting of Paris Hilton's face, peeking at passers-by in a mournfully seductive way from a torn opening in the wall. There is also a painting of an enormous rhinoceros barging its way through a breach in the wall, and I encounter billboard-size menus painted on the Wall. They offer:

BAHAMAS SEAFOOD, SHRIMPS, LOBSTER, BEEF FILLET,
GORDON BLUE *(spelled that way)*, DESSERT

Across the street, I notice a restaurant named The Wall Lounge. Flags from different countries flit in the breeze on its rooftop. I admire the owner's sense of humour, how he or she has made lemonade from their lot of lemons.

I want to walk the full length of the Wall in Bethlehem and document all the art and graffiti, but our time here is up. Before we board a waiting bus nearby, two Palestinian men approach us, selling colourful, embroidered bags. One of them comes directly to me, holding out a bag. For some reason, everywhere I have travelled (the Middle East, India, Africa), vendors and beggars gravitate towards me. I am typically the one to be singled out from my group of fellow travellers. Sometimes, I have to wonder if they see "soft-hearted loser" tattooed on my forehead.

I take the bag from him and run my finger over the stitching, thinking it would make a nice gift for a friend.

"My mother made it," the man says, as if sensing that particular detail would make a difference to me.

It does.

"For you, madam, 50 shekels."

"*Tayib*, okay."

Even though I only half-believe his story, I imagine his elderly mother hunched over in a chair, her gnarly fingers embroidering geometric patterns on a piece of fabric.

How can I refuse?

I hand him 50 shekels (about $15 Canadian).

Back on the bus, I examine the bag more closely and notice a small white tag sewn on the inside that has Hebrew writing. Ordinarily, I would be upset by the deception, but I'm not. How can I expect the man to be honest while the actual impact and truth behind the Wall is being suppressed, while his land, livelihood and chance of living a peaceful life continue to be stolen from him and justified through lies?

Provocative, omnipresent and oppressive, the Wall has also become a billboard, a cry of protest, in multiple languages, about injustice, about a pained people, whose yearning for freedom will never disappear, about a people refusing to give up or remain voiceless.

THIRTEEN

Keeping Hope Alive in Aida Refugee Camp

IF THE OLIVE TREES KNEW WHO PLANTED THEM,
THEIR OIL WOULD TURN INTO TEARS.

Graffiti on Cement Fence, Inside Aida Refugee Camp
Source Unknown

I t's windless. The smell of misery hangs in the air, smouldering garbage mingled with the stench of urine, fermenting fruit and a dead dog.

Late in the afternoon, we are walking alongside the Wall at the northern edge of Aida camp, one of three Palestinian refugee camps in the Bethlehem area. Located just two kilometres north of Bethlehem, the camp is completely surrounded by colossal concrete walls. Our guide Jalal, a resident of Aida, leads the olive pickers east along a road running parallel to the Wall. Between the road and the Wall is a strip of ground, the camp's garbage dump, where clumps of weeds poke through the piles of garbage and chunks of cement. Navy-coloured garbage bins labelled, "UN," burp up clouds of chemical-smelling smoke.

"The UN, who is responsible for providing services to the refugee camp, is currently on strike," Jalal explains.

It hits me as strange. *How can this be? Is there a statutory ordinance enabling the United Nations to strike?*

The United Nations established Aida camp in 1950. Its name means,

"To return." This was supposed to be a temporary place to accommodate Palestinians who were driven from their homes in 1948 to make way for a Jewish state. The refugees lived in tents at first, thinking they would be able to return their villages in a few weeks. The tents in Aida camp are long gone and have been replaced with a mishmash of cement and stone houses. About 5,000 Palestinians, Christians and Muslims, now live here. Their numbers have grown since it was created, but the designated camp boundaries have stayed the same. The refugees came from 17 different villages that all became part of Israel. Like hundreds of other Palestinian communities, Israel depopulated them and obliterated them from the modern map and annals of time. For over 60 years, generations of refugees have been living in this crowded and impoverished place. To me, calling Aida a prison camp would be more apt.

Here, at the edge of the camp, peace activists have used the entire height of the Wall, over eight metres, as their canvas. I am mesmerized as we pass one giant, satirical painting after another—non-violent protests against Israel's military occupation. In a painting of a dinosaur-sized cockroach knocking over the Wall, the rectangular concrete slabs topple like dominoes. Scrawled on the cockroach's body is:

THE OPPRESSED HAVE BECOME THE OPPRESSORS.

ZIONISM IS RACISM.

I recognize a Bansky painting depicting a string of people going up a black escalator that rises from the earth at the base of the Wall to its top. Next to it is an enormous blue-coloured cartoon of a pudgy boy, who is wearing glasses and crawling on the ground, saying,

I LOVE ANIMATION.

I am not clear about the meaning. Beside this cartoon, in white capital letters, is the word:

CAPTIVATING.

It stands out. The letters measure two metres high and run more than 20 metres in length near the top of the Wall. I notice there is a period after the word and ponder the irony in this statement that sums up Aida refugee camp. I wonder, too, how the activists climb high enough to produce such massive paintings. I am fascinated by the courage it takes to scale the colossal wall, under the watchful eye of Israeli soldiers stationed at all times inside the nearby watchtower.

Some of us walk over to the base of the Wall to get a closer look at the multi-lingual graffiti overtop the giant murals. We have to tread cautiously over the compacted layers of garbage. The bottom part of the Wall that is within our reach is layered with graffiti. In some places, newer graffiti covers portions of older musings, marks and messages. Elsewhere along the Wall, the messages stand out:

THIS IS A LAND GRAB.

GOD IS LOVE.

A COUNTRY IS NOT WHAT IT DOES, BUT ALSO WHAT IT TOLERATES.

Across from the garbage dump, on the other side of the road, is a three-story concrete building. Clearly built in stages over time, I notice that each level of the building is a different shade of taupe. It has small windows and doors and its sides are covered in graffiti. Laundry hangs to dry outside windows and balconies. With all the dust and acrid smoke in the air, even clothes are robbed of smelling clean.

Amina and I cross the garbage dump and walk over to the building. On a second-floor balcony, a 20-something-looking Palestinian man sits under strings of laundry, watching us. We exchange *salaams* from the street below.

"Where are you from?" he asks. It is the first thing the locals are curious about, regardless of where I travel.

"A Moroccan from the Netherlands," I say, pointing to Amina, knowing she does not speak Arabic. "And, I'm a Lebanese Canadian."

"*Ahlan,*" he says, smiling.

At times, I am unsure of how I will be received, especially coming from Canada. The Canadian Prime Minister, Steven Harper, a staunch supporter of Israel, voted against UN resolutions that called for a cease-fire when Israel waged war on Lebanon in 2006 and again voted "No" in 2008 when Israel bombed and blockaded Gaza. His vote essentially said "no" to averting further bloodshed. So, I am always pleasantly surprised when a Palestinian does not hold those actions against me. The opposite is true. Everywhere I go,

Palestinians are welcoming, generous and gracious.

"May I take your photograph?" I ask.

"Go ahead."

He straightens and beams for the camera.

He says, "I recently got married. You're welcome to come inside and meet my wife." He motions for us to come up.

"*Shukrun*, it would be our pleasure," I say, and glance at Amina, who is nodding excitedly in agreement. "But we can't stay long."

We enter the building's lobby at ground level. Its walls are covered with Arabic graffiti, which continues up the walls of the stairwell to the second floor. The newlyweds meet us outside the door of their apartment.

"This is my wife Maya."

The man wraps his arm around his pretty, young bride, who smiles shyly.

"What brings you to Palestine?" he asks us.

"We are volunteers, part of a group who came from around the world to help Palestinians with the olive harvest," I reply.

They both smile.

"My wife and I really appreciate other Arabs who care enough to come to Palestine and stand in solidarity with us."

Amina's face reddens when I translate for her.

"My family was originally from the village of Beit Hamser," he tells us. "My wife's family fled here from Jerusalem. We were born and raised here."

Amina holds the camera as I pose with the couple. I do the same for her. I am amazed at how they can maintain the motivation to get out of bed in the morning and be greeted by concrete walls and a garbage dump, knowing the day only promises the same suffering as yesterday.

Being a refugee, "the largest and longest-standing refugee crises in the world," is the story of this young couple's life. I wish it was a one-of-a-kind story, but it is not. It is the same story for generations of Palestinians. Decades of displacement and dispossession, living under military occupation, denied your human rights, herded into refugee camps and forgotten. Despite this, they continue to have hope in their ever-shrinking, oppressive world. They attend school, work, get married and have children.

Where does that primordial, unseen strength come from?

Hope is a curious state and attitude. Amorphous. How can hope flourish in a refugee camp? Perhaps hope is all they have left, all one really has.

Before long, I hear one of the organizers yelling out our names.

"We have to go," I say, embracing Maya. "It was nice meeting you."

We rejoin our group. The road slopes downhill. Jalal points to a spot further down, next to the Wall where residents decided to greet Pope Benedict during his planned one-hour visit to Aida camp earlier this year on May 13, 2009.

"The people of the camp were hoping that the Pope's visit would raise awareness of the suffering of Palestinians," he explains.

Residents cleaned a rectangular area sandwiched between the Wall and the road. They covered the ground with a layer of concrete and built a platform for the Pope to speak from. The spot next to the Wall and the burning bins of garbage nearby is not a place befitting a Pope, but open space is non-existent in Aida, where a community of 5,000 people is crammed into an area less than one square kilometre in size. There are no open spaces capable of holding the more than a thousand people, Muslims and Christians alike, who would have shown up to celebrate the Pope's visit. In the end, Israeli authorities refused to allow Aida residents to welcome the Pope in this location, forcing event organizers to relocate to the only school in the camp.

I can appreciate why Israeli officials objected to this spot. For a moment, I visualize the Pope standing on the stage, spreading the teachings of the Prince of Peace, facing a garbage dump, flanked on one side by the Wall and Aida refugee camp on the other. I wonder how Pope Benedict felt when he visited the place; being German, he must have appreciated the impact of a separation barrier.

In the background, behind where the Pope would have stood, a watchtower protrudes above the Wall. Both have become one, gigantic canvas. The natural blue sky and the painted sky blend together, appearing as one stretch. In the background of the actual painting, a Palestinian village is ablaze, surrounded by Israeli tanks. Young men resist by throwing stones at the tanks. In the foreground, two soldiers lead a blindfolded Palestinian away.

We continue walking east towards one of the entrances to Aida camp. A mud fence three metres tall marks its northern edge and is decorated in colourful paintings: pastoral scenes depicting a former way of life — people harvesting fields of ripened wheat, a woman climbing a ladder to pick an olive tree, three children standing next to their mother as she balances a water jug on her head. I pause to gaze at them. The simplistic drawings remind me of illustrations found in children's books. They strike a chord with me. I see my mother in them. They speak to her former way of life in Lebanon, where as a young mother she too balanced a water jug on her head, harvested wheat by hand and climbed ladders to get to the ripened olives.

We reach an entrance where a two-tonne replica of a key lies sideways on top of a gate, which has been built over the street. The gate is reddish-brown and shaped like a keyhole.

Not For Sale

is inscribed on the key in Arabic and English. It is a constant reminder and symbol of the displacement of Palestinians. It embodies their undiminished desire to return to their homes and villages. They have kept the keys to their former homes, passing them down from generation to generation for more than sixty years, trying to "keep hope alive," which is also the mantra of the Alternative Tourism Group.

We enter Aida camp through a different entrance leading to a newer section. The paintings on the six-metre-high concrete fence lining the street pull me in, provoking emotions: anger, frustration, sadness. There is a painting of an army jeep and soldiers pointing their guns at a group of demonstrators carrying flags that read:

Right of Return for All Generations

and The Wall Must Fall

It is as though I'm walking through an outdoor living museum. Each section of fence is dedicated to a different village, which Palestinians used to call home. I'm reminded of the ancient Egyptians who etched their stories, history and traditions on the walls of tombs and temples. So, too, the Palestinians in Aida continue to record their history, values and aspirations. One section of fence bears a childlike painting of an olive tree. Another section of fence has the map of Palestine. Its caption says:

WE WILL RETURN

and lists former Palestinian villages and cities: Zakariyah, Beit Jebreen, Ajoor and others. Palestinians believe they have the right to return to their villages.

Jalal stops beside it. "Israel claims to be the inheritors of the real Jews," he says. "They have the right after more than 2,000 years to return. Why not the Palestinians?"

He mentions that the universal right to return home is enshrined in international law under various provisions of the 1948 Universal Declaration of Human Rights and Resolution 194 of the United Nations General Assembly.

We follow a road littered with paper and plastic bags, passing newer two- and three-story, white stone houses with wrought-iron gates and rounded balconies, next to half-built homes with bunches of rebar sticking out of their flat roofs. An elderly woman wearing a long white *hijab* shuffles along the street. Head down, slightly hunched, hands clenched behind her back, she looks as if she is carrying the weight of the world on her shoulders.

The atmosphere is calm as we make our way through an older section of Aida camp. But it is not always like this. Residents never know *when* Israeli soldiers will come — only that they *will* come.

Jalal tells us, "The Israeli army routinely targets Aida camp, raiding with tanks and armed soldiers, terrorizing us in the middle of the night with tear gas, wild dogs and live ammunition.

"Ask any kid. Most have been shot with tear gas. Most have had a family member who was killed or jailed."

Several dust-stained boys are kicking a deflated soccer ball around to one side of the street. They stop playing when they notice us, stare as we pass them.

Jalal points out homes pockmarked from bullets shot by snipers stationed at Rachel's Tomb nearby. Then he directs our attention to the roof of another house.

"That's where Israeli soldiers shot and killed a 10-year-old Palestinian boy as he played with his pet pigeons," he tells the group.

I feel as if I have been kicked while I was already down.

We continue walking through Aida camp. There are no sidewalks or gardens. Most homes appear to have been built over time. The upper floors are newer, with white stone facades. Here, the streets are too narrow for cars to pass through. Houses, crammed together, begin at the edge of the winding alleys and rise up several levels. A jumble of electrical wires criss-crosses overhead. Graffiti is everywhere: on the exterior walls of homes and businesses, on light posts and garbage bins. A young boy is walking on the road about 20 metres ahead of the group, pulling his younger brother along with one hand and carrying a plastic bag in the other. A skinny, spotted cat darts across our path. Another young boy sits alone on his front step at the edge of the street, looking painfully bored.

"There is no room — except up," Jalal says. "Even the cemetery is full. There is no room. Not even for the dead."

A group of children approach us, curious, friendly and full of energy. Some notice me holding a camera and pose for photographs. They crowd around me and giggle when I show them their pictures.

"Do you like school?" I ask them.

Their eyes widen when they hear me speak Arabic. Most of them nod enthusiastically.

"What do you want to be when you grow up, *habibbati*?"

They excitedly share their dreams of becoming doctors, journalists and computer engineers.

A quiet boy with green eyes and long eyelashes pipes up. "I want to be a truck driver!" "Just like my father."

The other children break out in laughter.

As we pass by homes and small shops, the people of Aida receive us with smiles and say *salaam* or *ahlan*. One lady invites me inside for tea or coffee. I mention that I am with a large group.

"That's not a problem," she says without hesitation. "Tell them they are all welcome."

I know she means it.

On our way out of Aida refugee camp, one of the six women from Korea stops at a house to talk with an elderly Palestinian man. He is resting on a small stool just outside an open door.

"Welcome," he says, extending his hand to her, delighted with the attention. He smiles, showing missing front teeth. Though neither of them can speak the other's language, they manage to communicate, comprehend each other from their gestures and broken English. I stand to the side. There is no need to step in and translate.

"Thank you for visiting us in Aida," he says, and kisses her hand.

Her face reddens.

"You, from where? China?"

"No. Korea," she says in a soft voice.

"Korea?" his voice booms louder by comparison.

They both nod in unison, smiling. She turns to me.

"Please. Can you take a photo?"

She hands me her camera and crouches down beside him while I take several pictures, sensing that she will always remember this moment.

I look over my shoulder at him one last time as we leave, also sensing that I will never forget this place. Aida refugee camp is largely veiled from world view. Generations of Palestinians are trapped behind walls and watchtowers, forsaken refugees, still stateless, still gripping the keys to their former homes, still hoping to return, amid the lingering smells of burning garbage.

FOURTEEN

The Old City of Hebron

You will SEE firsthand what is going on in Palestine and Israel.
If a picture is worth a thousand words, then an experience is worth
a thousand pictures.

"Study and Fact Finding Tours"
Holy Land Trust, February 2011

Our busload of volunteer olive pickers arrives in Hebron early in the morning for a day-long tour. This ancient city is home to about 160,000 indigenous Palestinians and 800 Jewish settlers who have seized key parts of the city. There are more than 2,000 Israeli soldiers, more than two soldiers for every Jewish settler, and hundreds of police stationed here to protect the settlers, many of whom are also heavily armed. For me, Hebron is the epitome of lawlessness.

A tall, slim man is waiting for us in the middle of a street near an Israeli checkpoint.

"My name is Omar. I am Palestinian," he says, smiling after everyone has gotten off the bus and congregated around him. "I will be taking you through the old city of Hebron where I live."

I listen to him while eyeing the checkpoint only 20 metres away, a beige trailer-like structure blocking the street ahead. The sidewalks on either side of it are blocked by iron gates. Through the windows, I see the silhouettes of several soldiers inside, checking the IDs of a few tourist-looking people wanting to get to the other side. It is a familiar sight, as is the street lined on both sides with three-story stone buildings. Rusted turquoise-coloured awnings hang over the doors of abandoned business shops on the ground level. The windows of the upper residential levels are covered with metal bars for protection from stones and garbage thrown up at Palestinians by Jewish settlers. There is Arabic graffiti everywhere. It occurs to me that I am standing on Shuhada Street, a major road running east-west through the center of Hebron. Israel "sterilized" and deemed it off-limits to Palestinians in 2002.

Memories of the autumn of 2009 flood back. Only a year ago, I walked the length of Shuhada Street on the other side of the same checkpoint with members of the Arab-Jewish Women's Peace Coalition during a tour hosted by Breaking the Silence. This time, our guide and the representatives from the Alternative Tourism Group are Palestinians, who are barred from walking on Shuhada Street.

We follow our guide north to a commercial area. In contrast to Shuhada Street only a couple of blocks away, which has now become a ghost town, this part of Hebron is alive and bustling with Palestinian shoppers. I am excited to be back in the "City of the Patriarchs," a rare chance, relatively speaking, to see another side of it. I hang back at the tail end of the group, as we walk down the middle of a street edged on both sides with shops selling a multitude of things. Men's shirts and scarves hang on ropes above our heads, and tables brim with children's toys, stuffed animals and soccer balls. Shop owners stand behind tables covered with bins full of different coloured candy and nuts. They watch as I take photographs of the sacks of macaroni noodles, lentils and onions on the ground next to their tables. I am uplifted by the sensory overload.

My spirit is soon dampened, however, when we reach the steel barricade built across the street, turning it into a dead end. One man has set up shop here, using the wall of iron beams to hang an assortment of women's dresses. We continue on through a residential area, passing intersecting streets that the Israeli army has closed off with metal gates. Some streets are blocked by large concrete slabs or rows of rusted barrels filled with cement. I assume the connecting network of smaller side roads all lead to the forbidden Shuhada Street.

"Israel installed iron gates across 22 entrances to Shuhada Street," Omar tells us. "It divided the city in half. Palestinians living north of this street now have to make a 10-kilometre detour to see their families who live to the south of it, just several blocks away."

I hear the frustration in his voice.

"The settlers are free to move about, but the Palestinians need permission from the Israeli army for every turn. Israel's objective is to make life hard. It is a silent deportation. It is happening all over the Occupied Palestinian Territories."

A short while later, we are in the old city, the most ancient part of Hebron. It saddens me to see evidence of the takeover of this 900-year-old place, street by street and house by house. Jewish settlers have established five small illegal settlements here. We stroll down a bustling street where one settlement has been built on top of the Palestinian market. The ground levels on either side of the street are packed with Palestinian-owned shops and stalls. The floors above the shops are the settlement. Jewish settlers have either seized the upper levels of Palestinian-owned buildings or built extensions overtop the Palestinian shops. Palestinian residents and shop owners had to construct metal nets over the street for protection, to catch the garbage and other debris thrown down at them by settlers.

I look up in disbelief at the roof of metal beams and mesh above me, and the things it has caught: rocks, bricks, a muddy one-armed doll with its eyes poked out, dirty diapers, a plastic lawn chair, bottles, cardboard and other garbage. It seems unreal, but it is very real. This is the reality for Palestinians living and working here.

Our guide stops to one side of the street and we gather around him.

"The net protects us from some things," he says wearily. "Now the settlers throw eggs, bottles of urine, bleach."

I point my camera up, zoom in for a closer look through the openings in the garbage net and photograph the Israeli soldiers standing on the rooftops of buildings, their guns aimed down on us. Security cameras are also mounted on rooftops, capturing the action on the street below.

"The settlers, mainly from the States — Florida — want to rebuild the Jewish community in Hebron," Omar says. "They intend to empty the area of Palestinians and take the entire city. They believe they have a divine right to do so."

As we stand here listening to him, I feel something drop on my head. Startled, our group scurries in different directions. I run my hand over my hair, realizing we have been pelted with dirt from one of the homes overlooking the street, likely by a settler.

"Let's move on," Omar says, leading us away from the market to a residential area. He stops at another dead end. Here, the narrow street is blocked with rolls of razor wire and littered with garbage. Running parallel to it is a metal fence. I look up the hill to my right at another Jewish settlement. It is easy to spot with its newer stone buildings and green lawns.

We reach an ancient *souk*, a market. It is like entering a labyrinth with its open-air streets and cave-like tunnels. Shops line both sides of the dim, narrow alleyways of cobble-stone streets and domed stone ceilings. Vendors trying to eke a living stand beside sacks of green olives and pails of pickled grape leaves, pickled peppers and cauliflower dyed bright pink by using beets. Further along, a vendor sells cheap costume jewellery next to a vendor selling *rababbis*, Arabic zithers, beside a shop offering dried figs, roasted watermelon seeds and a variety of other foods. There is a surprise around every turn. The whole experience is a surprise. I straggle behind the group, taking photographs of what some of the vendors are selling, sometimes getting curious looks, especially when I aim my camera at the stainless steel bowls sitting on a table, filled with raw chicken hearts, kidneys and dangling genitalia of, I am guessing, bulls. A middle-aged man behind one table continues to watch me as I turn my attention to a salmon-coloured t-shirt hanging from a rafter above his table of raw organs.

"*Marhaba*," I say to him.

"*Ahlan*," he replies. His brows rise in surprise upon hearing me speak Arabic.

On the front of the t-shirt is a drawing of Handala. I snap a photograph of it.

"It's not for sale," the man tells me with a slight smile.

I suspect he knows I already know that. The shirt is oil-stained in several places. It is well-worn and hangs here as a statement. I want to tell him that I appreciate why he has put a drawing of Handala in his stall, that I understand the importance of this cartoon character. He is an icon of non-violent resistance, a reminder that Palestinian refugees will never give up wanting and fighting for their universal right to return home.

I loiter by his stall for a few minutes, adjusting my camera settings absentmindedly. Neither of us speaks. There's no need for words.

"*Ma'alsalaama*," I say, finally waving goodbye.

"*Ma'alsalaama.*"

He nods, and places his hand simultaneously against his chest in respect. I am touched; he does not even know my name.

I catch up to the group, feeling as if I could easily get lost as we twist and turn along the narrow alleyways. Here, there are no spaces between the dilapidated homes on either side. Decay and soot cover the walls; rusting metal doors are fronted with garbage. We encounter more closed streets. Several young boys congregate near one that is barricaded by sheets of metal that have been cut and welded together to fit the tunnel-like street. Further down another street, we come across a boy about 12 years old standing with a soccer ball tucked under his arm, watching us as we walk by. The dim alley is his playground, his world. There is a nervous, urgent energy to this hovel-like place. A weariness. A longing for normalcy. A waning hope. By contrast, the problems in my own life now seem insignificant.

I saw him for a few minutes in 2009, and never learned his name, but there is no forgetting his darkly-tanned, triangular face and hazel eyes. This time, he is roaming the ancient alleys of Hebron with an armful of colourfully embroidered handbags with JERUSALEM stitched across them in red. And, of the hundreds of people I met last year, I knew I would never forget him, and thought it unlikely I would ever see him again. He became a memory, that young, skinny Palestinian living in Hebron, who wore a t-shirt that said:

PEACE WILL COME. WHY NOT NOW?

The teenager wore a permanent smile during our brief encounter, despite the fact that he lived like a prisoner. He was in need of money yet generously gave me a beaded bracelet. I still have it.

I stay back, watching him as he approaches our group, wondering if he will remember me. His pushiness is off-putting and there are no takers in our group, but he refuses to take "No, thank you," for an answer. For him, "*La Shukrun*" means "maybe in a few minutes." He is persistent and follows our group, showing up out of nowhere as we meander through the ancient alleys. At one point, Bisan, an advocacy and communication officer with the Alternative Tourism Group, stops and faces him.

"*Khalas.* Enough. You are being a pest," she says to him in her usual polite tone. "Leave us alone."

But, that does little to discourage him.

"Fifty shekels," he pleads, holding up an embroidered bag for us to see.

"We just passed a shop selling the same bags for only 30 shekels," I make the mistake of telling one of the women in our group. He understands me, and when no one buys a handbag from him, he becomes angry.

"They burned my house, but we have God," he repeats, looking to the sky.

He glares at me. "It's your entire fault. You ruined my chances."

"*Asfee habibi,*" I say, trying to apologize. "I met you last year. Don't you remember me? You gave me a beaded bracelet."

He looks me in the eye. "I see many tourists and visitors."

"I'm sure you do. I never forgot you," I say, smiling. "You were wearing a t-shirt with the message, 'Peace will come. Why not now?'"

But he looks unimpressed. Suddenly, I hear someone, his friend I assume, yell out. "ISLAM!"

He turns and heads towards him, still miffed. I feel bad, but I finally learned his name. It is indeed a small world, I think, to cross paths with Islam again. Last year I left him with a smile on his face, this time, a scowl.

—⁊—

Our guide, Omar, stops outside a drab three-story stone building where the Awawi family lives. We gather around him. He explains that in 1997, Jewish settlers took over the rooftop, a two-story at the time. They built a third floor on top and moved in. For protection, they also built a military watchtower above the extension, which is continuously manned by soldiers.

"Follow me, please," he tells our group.

We enter a dark, narrow stairwell charred by fire, and climb a narrow flight of stairs. On the second level, a young boy, who appears to be about six years old, stands outside a low doorway. As we shuffle up the stairs past him, he holds out a newborn baby wrapped in a blanket, trying to get our attention. I assume the baby is a sibling and worry he might drop it. An older boy soon comes to the door, ushers the youngster back inside without looking at us and closes the door. We continue up the winding stone stairs to the flat rooftop of the settler extension.

I appreciate the bird's-eye-view of part of the old city of Hebron. The Awawi home sits on a slope and is surrounded on three sides by settler homes. I scan the hilly landscape. It is easy to spot Palestinian homes; metal beams stretched across arched windows, water tanks, in multiples of two and three, sprout from rooftops, whereas the settlers have the resources to build their water and sewage systems underground. A military base on top of a hill overlooks us. There is a Muslim cemetery to one side and Jewish settlements scattered in the Palestinian neighbourhood.

We are not alone. Only a few metres away, a bored-looking soldier leans against a watchtower built to one side of the Awawi rooftop. He observes us without approaching. As I look around me, I realize our group is being watched from all angles. It is hard not to notice the soldiers stationed on rooftops around us. I know they are here to protect the settlers, but it is clear who needs protection from whom. The soldiers stand with their guns, outside tiny shelters made of wood and corrugated iron roofs that have been draped with green camouflage netting. I notice there are flood lights to help them see at night and cameras pointing down on the streets below, where I see squads of soldiers patrolling the neighbourhood. A sickness prowls the streets, saturates the air.

I feel as if I am in a war zone.

Ordinarily, I would be fearful of getting shot at for taking photographs of military installations and soldiers, but this is a braver moment for me. Fear takes a back seat as I capture as many images as I can. Many of the olive pickers do the same.

Three members of the Palestinian student delegation from Denmark, who joined our tour, pose for photographs with the military outpost in the background. They hoist the Palestinian flag above their heads proudly, laughing, giving the peace sign. I think about the notion of identity and the territorial imperative that binds Palestinians to this land. Even though their parents and grandparents have lived for decades in the Diaspora, and even though these students are seeing Palestine for the first time, they still say things like, "This is our land."

Bisan notices and walks over to them. "Please, put the flag away," she says, clearly wanting to avoid a confrontation with soldiers and the settlers.

"The settlers have made life unbearable for the Awawi family," she explains, motioning for us to gather around her. "On numerous occasions, they set fire to the house — while the family of ten was still inside. The Awawi children are traumatized. One daughter developed an uncontrolled bladder problem; another daughter has been receiving psychiatric treatment from Doctors Without Borders. Their mother suffered a miscarriage because the settlers would not allow her to leave her house for medical help when she began having abdominal pain."

She pauses for a second before continuing. Her eyes have that far-away look.

"And the most painful story is when the settlers locked the husband and wife inside their house and blocked the door with sand bags to prevent the children from entering their home. The Awawi children were forced to sleep with other family members for three days.

"This family's story is documented in many places," she says, finally.

—⁂—

We come to the end of a dark alley that leads to the Ibrahimi Mosque, or Tomb of the Patriarchs. We wait our turn in line to go through the checkpoint. There are several soldiers manning it. One of them sits inside a cubicle, controlling the turnstile. The buzzing as he presses a button to allow a few people through at a time, and the clanging and clicking of the metal turnstiles soon become irritating. I am relieved when I come out the other side of the barrier, where I wait in a stone courtyard in front of the Ibrahimi Mosque until the last of our group passes through the x-ray machine and turnstiles.

I stare up at part of the ancient exterior wall surrounding the rectangular complex. Claimed by some to have been built by Herod the Great, the outside walls are 15 metres high and made of massive stone blocks. The plainness of the structure is uninviting, and if you ignore the two stone minarets towering above it, the structure resembles a medieval castle (minus the moat) rather than a mosque. It does not feel like a sanctuary or sacred place with all the soldiers and checkpoints. Despite this, I am excited to have the chance to go inside the Muslim section. The complex was built over a cave containing the tombs of the common patriarchs and matriarchs of Christians, Muslims and Jews. Obviously, it is only fitting that all peoples have access. Currently, what lies within the foreboding-looking walls is divided into part synagogue-part mosque, separated by a wooden interior wall.

To the left is the Muslim entrance, where there is another Israeli checkpoint: a metal detector to go through and a search by several soldiers before entry. I watch as they check inside the bags of the Muslim worshippers. To the right is a stone walkway that zigzags up, a separate entrance for Jewish people, where a group of Jewish worshippers make their way into the synagogue part of the complex, suffering no obstacles.

Finally, we have permission to go inside.

"You are free to roam around on our own," Omar tells us. "Let's meet back here in two hours."

After the soldier searches through my camera bag, I climb a long flight of stone steps. At the top, two more soldiers stand watch as I enter through a door on the right, where a Muslim man hands out long, brown robes to the women in our group. I slip mine over my clothes and enter the Djaouliyeh

Mosque portion of the complex. Sandalwood incense wafts through the air, and immediately I feel a peaceful, soothing energy. The spacious room is adorned with white marble columns that support graceful archways. Red carpet with geometric patterns covers the floor. It is not prayer time yet. Several men are sitting on the floor to one side, reading. Other visitors mill about. I cannot help but remember that a massacre occurred on this spot in 1994. It feels strange, almost uncomfortable, to be standing where Baruch Goldstein, a Jewish doctor, gunned down 29 Palestinian Muslims as they were prostrating in prayer. Over a hundred other worshippers were also injured.

Sadly, it was not the only human slaughter in Hebron's more recent times. In 1929, increasing Jewish immigration to Palestine led to violence. Some Palestinians in Hebron went on a murderous riot, killing dozens of Jewish people. It was a cycle of violence begetting violence.

I turn my attention to the mosque's dome ceiling, painted in a variety of pastel colours, struggling to keep the hood of my robe from slipping off and exposing my hair, not wanting to offend any worshipper. From the mosque, I walk through a stone passageway to a central room. Straight ahead of me, in a small room, is a cenotaph. A sign in Arabic tells me it belongs to Sarah, Prophet Abraham's wife. I peer through the green-painted metal mesh covering the room's window at the coffin-shaped box, which is draped in green cloth embroidered with Qur'anic verses. This marks the spot where, in the caverns directly below, the remains of Sarah are reportedly buried.

I continue easterly, where I come to a courtyard that leads to octagonal-shaped rooms that contain the cenotaphs of Jacob and Leah. Further east I enter another prayer hall, known as the Al-Is'haqeyyah Mosque or Great Mosque, where I find Isaac and Rebecca's. They are not covered with a decorative cloth like the others. The rectangular stone monuments are painted with red and white horizontal stripes, and sit in the middle of the prayer hall.

In the center of the complex, in a small room off the women's mosque, is the cenotaph of Abraham. There are green metal bars across the window of the small room. A flat boulder with an indentation catches my eye. Many believe that Adam, of Adam and Eve, prayed here so often that he left his footprint in the stone. I am intrigued, but skeptical of that claim. Still it is overwhelming to be standing over the tombs of ancient, common ancestors, key Biblical and Qur'anic figures. I feel privileged, awe-struck.

I see Jewish worshippers peering into the same room through a barred-up window on the wall opposite me. The Arabic sign outside Abraham's cenotaph translates in English to, "Our master Abraham, chosen friend, peace be upon him."

I make my way back to the central prayer hall in the southeastern part of the complex. Across the room from Isaac and Rebecca's cenotaphs is an ornate marble, *mihrab*, a niche showing the direction of prayer. A *minbar*, wooden pulpit, is built overtop a narrow shaft leading to the cavern below, which is closed to visitors. On the floor, a decorative metal grate covers the shaft. I bend down on all fours and peer through the peep holes. I see several dim lights that do little to illuminate the dark abyss. I am not sure what I am supposed to see. I remain staring into the blackened nothing for a while and silently recite the *fatiha*.

After spending about an hour inside, enjoying the peaceful ambiance and with free time left, I make my way outside and head south, down a short road leading to Shuhada Street. At the end of it is another checkpoint, but before I get to it, a black Israeli soldier approaches me.

"Are there any Muslims in your group?"

He speaks with an American accent, catches me off guard, and I immediately think of Amina and some of the Danish students who are wearing *hijabs* and are visibly Muslim.

"It's not something I ask people about," I reply, shrugging my shoulders. "It's a private matter. Why do you need to know?"

He replies, "Because Muslims are not allowed."

I assume he means not allowed to walk on Shuhada Street. It bothers me that I cannot see his eyes, hidden behind dark, expensive sunglasses. I see my reflection on their mirrored surface. I'm aware of my calmness, surprised that I have no fear of him and I sense he knows that.

"How is that important?" I press, trying to carry on a conversation.

After a contemplative pause, he replies, "I'm just doing my job."

He walks away towards the checkpoint. I continue about a block to

Shuhada Street where I buy some scarves from one of the shops. That is when I notice a familiar face among a group of tourists.

"Yehuda!"

I realize immediately that I have shouted out his name at the surprise of seeing him again. He turns to face me, looking almost startled.

"Hello," I say, feeling slightly embarrassed. "I'm Carmen. I was here last year with the Arab-Jewish Women's Peace Coalition. We took a tour of Hebron with you."

It is clear from the blank stare Yehuda does not remember me, not that I expected him to. A few awkward seconds pass before his mobile phone rings.

"Good seeing you again," I wave goodbye, and head back to our meeting point outside the Ibrahimi Mosque.

I am pleased to know Yehuda is still bringing busloads of visitors to see this ancient place, where the past and present clash and collide. It has been said "a picture is worth a thousand words." Here, in Hebron, as some alternative tour companies promise, the experience is truly "worth a thousand pictures."

FIFTEEN

"Judaizing" the Old City of Jerusalem

I hope America wakes up before it's too late. They talk about democracy. No one believes them. No one trusts American foreign policy. We are starving because of that policy. Get rid of the occupation. Deal with the Palestinians as human beings, there would be no need for violence. It's not our hobby to be violent. I want to see my son grow up to be an engineer, doctor or pilot. The occupation is immoral. We are tired. We want to have nice dreams instead of nightmares.

Ali Jiddah, Tour Guide, Old City of Jerusalem

It feels as if we are trying to cross the border into a foreign country. We are on our way to tour the Old City of Jerusalem, but stuck in a line-up at a military checkpoint on the northern outskirts of Bethlehem. As our bus inches forward, I photograph the Wall through the window. It blocks the highway and snakes east over stony hills once covered in pine, hills taken and transformed to build the Har Homa settlement. The Wall segregates the city where they say Jesus, peace be upon him, was born, from the city where he was reportedly crucified and resurrected.

Hideous and oppressive, the bottom half of the Wall is covered with large paintings and graffiti in different languages. There is a drawing of a man's face, covered by the traditional Palestinian *kafiyee*, a black and white chequered scarf; only his large dark eyes stare hauntingly at passers-by. Beside him, in red letters, is the caption:

To exist is to resist.

Next to that is a painting of a lion, its fangs dug into a bleeding white dove.

After a half hour wait, our bus finally makes it to an enormous steel gate imbedded in the Wall. Our Palestinian driver hands his Israeli-mandated, magnetic ID through the window to the armed gatekeepers. He is one of the lucky ones who have a permit. Israel has barred most of the Palestinians I encountered from going to Jerusalem, including many of the olive harvest organizers.

"I'm taking a group of pilgrims to Jerusalem," our driver says, his head poking out the open window.

Seemingly unconvinced, two Israeli soldiers climb on board to check for themselves. Fingers curled around triggers of M16s, they stomp down the aisle to the back of the bus, where Amina is feigning sleep. A teal-coloured hijab frames her flawless, ivory complexion. She is the only visible Muslim on the bus.

"Your passport," one of the soldiers demands of her.

Amina yawns, trying not to look bothered. She digs into her bag, smiles sweetly as she surrenders her Dutch passport. After confirming our bus is not harbouring terrorists or attempting to smuggle unwanted or unauthorized Palestinians into Jerusalem, the soldier returns Amina's passport and the pair exit through the side door. The steel gate opens and we continue north to the Old City of Jerusalem, about 10 kilometres away.

Along the way, Kristel goes over the day's itinerary. She stands at the front of the bus facing us with a microphone in hand.

"Our guide is Ali, an African Palestinian from Chad and, among other sites, he will be taking us to the African Quarter of the Old City," she tells us.

This grabs my attention.

I've read various books about the Old City, visited it several times already, strolled its twisting alleys and bustling open markets, and walked its ramparts. I have not heard of the African Quarter, though, only the Christian, Jewish, Armenian and Muslim Quarters, whose names are based on the resident's ethnic and religious make-up. Yet, despite the names, there is a mingling of people, a mixing of past and present. I was pleased and somewhat surprised to encounter churches within the Muslim Quarter: Church of Flagellation, Saint Veronica Church and Virgin Mary's Birth Church. And much of the length of the Via Dolorosa lies in the Muslim Quarter. I also found the Al-Kabir Mosque and Mohareb Mosque in the Jewish Quarter, and the Church of the Holy Sepulchre and Omar Mosque standing side-by-side in the Christian Quarter.

But an African Quarter? How serendipitous!

We pour out of the bus. Kristel leads us through Dung Gate or Bab Al-Maghreb, which translates into "Moroccan Gate," one of seven gateways into the Old City. The modified stone archway in the ancient wall leads directly to the Jewish Quarter and the Western Wall. It also leads to Haram Al-Sharif, the Noble Sanctuary, the third most important holy site for Muslims and, among other things, contains the Dome of the Rock and the Al-Aqsa Mosque. Jews and Christians refer to the Noble Sanctuary area as Temple Mount. It is reportedly the location of Solomon's Temple, which the Romans destroyed in 70 AD. Located in the southeast corner of the Old City, it is arguably the most contested, controversial and coveted 40 acres of land on the planet.

Just north of Dung Gate, we come across three young Israeli men going in the opposite direction. They stop when they notice Kiwi, as some in our group have secretly nicknamed her because she is always eager to talk about New Zealand's kiwi, the equivalent of Canada's beaver. A 10-inch replica of a kiwi bird sits in a bright pink scarf tied around her neck. It often draws attention. The tall, red-headed one in the group is not interested in the bird, however. He fingers the beaded bracelet of a Palestinian flag, which Kiwi had placed around the bird's neck, and his smile disappears from under his multi-coloured *kippa*.

"What is this?" he asks her in an accusing tone.

"I got it in Bethlehem," she tells him.

"You shouldn't!" he scolds Kiwi. "There is no Palestine. The Holy Land is for Jews only."

He walks away with his friends leaving Kiwi and me standing there for a few seconds, still and speechless.

A rectangular esplanade built on a plateau, the Noble Sanctuary has its own stone walls and series of gates. Our group reaches an L-shaped ramp leading to the only non-Muslim entrance to the Noble Sanctuary, also named Al-Maghreb Gate. It looks relatively new. Two young Israeli soldiers sit on white plastic lawn chairs at the end of the north-south section of the ramp. A string of Israeli flags hangs above their heads. They eye each one of us from head to toe as we file past them.

Our guide, Ali, is waiting for us in an open courtyard, sitting in the shade of a lone olive tree. He is wearing a brown hat and blue golf shirt. He is clean-shaven except for a short, salt-and-pepper moustache that stands out against his dark skin.

"I live in the African Quarter, which you will not find on any map," he says. His soft voice does not carry far, so we gather close around him as he gives us a brief history of the African Quarter.

The ancestors of the almost 100 families who currently live in the African Quarter came to Palestine from Chad, Nigeria, Senegal and Sudan. Many of them visited the Old City on their way to Mecca in Saudi Arabia where they were going to perform the Haj. Some stayed in Jerusalem; others settled elsewhere in Palestine, places like Jenin and Jericho, marrying local Palestinians and adopting the Arabic language and culture.

"My father is from Chad and my mother is a Palestinian from Gaza," he tells us. "I'm a second generation African Palestinian."

What became the African Quarter, two large buildings facing each other near the western walls of the Noble Sanctuary, was built by the Mamluks in the 1300s as guest houses for pilgrims. The buildings were later converted into a prison during the Arab revolt in 1917 against the ruling Turks before a Sheik gave the buildings to the African pilgrims, who remained in the Old City and eventually became "guardians" of the Dome of the Rock and the Al-Aqsa Mosque given the proximity of the African Quarter to Dung Gate.

We follow Ali east across a stone courtyard towards the Al-Aqsa Mosque. He has a tall, thin frame and leans on a silver crutch. To our right, rows of Corinthian pillars about a metre high resist the hot sun as they have for centuries. Ali stops and turns to face us.

"In 2001, Ariel Sharon came through the Maghreb Gate, the same gate you did," he says, pointing. "He came with a thousand soldiers. They marched across this courtyard where we are walking and barged their way inside the Al-Aqsa Mosque while people prayed."

This act provoked the Second Intifada. It feels strange to be walking the same path as Ariel Sharon, who now lies comatose from a stroke in a hospital, neither dead nor alive. This former Prime Minister of Israel was found to be responsible for the 1982 massacres in the Palestinian refugee camps of Sabra and Shatila in Lebanon by Christian militias.

We come to the north side of the Al-Aqsa Mosque. Its beige façade has seven stone arches supporting an open porch that runs along its entire length and leads to seven doors all painted forest green.

"It holds over 5,000 people," Ali informs us. "It is the largest mosque in Jerusalem."

I am seeing it up close for the first time, even though this is not my first visit to the Noble Sanctuary. Little remains of the original structure that was built in the early part of the eighth century. It has been damaged by several earthquakes, then restored and expanded by the various occupiers of the day. I gaze at it, thinking how unremarkable-looking it is compared to other mosques I've seen elsewhere. Its lead-covered dome is black from oxidation, offsetting its plainness. I feel compelled to go inside and pray, but I do not want to hold up the group.

We head north along a walkway lined on both sides with cedars. We pass the al-Kas (the cup) Fountain, a place where people perform ablutions before praying, and climb wide stairs to a graceful archway, one of several stone archways leading to a platform where the Dome of the Rock sits. Completed in 691 AD, the beautiful, octagon-shaped edifice is topped by a gold-plated dome. Its exterior bottom third is covered in white marble. The remainder is adorned in deep indigo and turquoise majolica tiles.

The courtyard surrounding the Dome of the Rock is busy with locals and tourists, yet the atmosphere is calm and peaceful. It is often mistaken for a mosque, but it is actually a shrine, though Muslims do pray inside. It was built to protect a rock considered sacred by Jews, Christians and Muslims. The rock is believed by some to be the "holiest of holy." It is the place where Abraham bound his son for sacrifice before God intervened, and where the souls of the dead will gather on Judgement Day. Some say it marks the center of the earth, where Mohammed ascended on his Night Journey. Some believe this is where the world will end, the Final Countdown to Armageddon, where the Third Temple will be built, meaning this beautiful edifice will be destroyed.

I refuse to believe this is where the world will end. Instead, I choose to think the Noble Sanctuary deserves to be designated and protected as a world heritage site, if it isn't already.

Several of the Palestinian students from Denmark, who joined the international group of volunteer olive pickers, pose with the Palestinian flag. Some tourists stop to take their photographs. An Israeli policeman notices.

"Put that flag away," he orders, which they do.

Then he turns his attention to Bertrand, a French activist. "Take that off," he points to the *kafiyee* wrapped around Bertrand's neck.

"No," Bertrand replies, shakes his head and walks away. The policeman retreats to his post.

Ali eases himself onto a chair outside the west door of the Dome of the Rock. "I'm going to wait for Amina. She's inside praying," he says to his assistant, Farah, a 16-year-old Palestinian boy. "Take the group to Al-Qattanin Market for a refreshment break."

Ali points to the Al-Qattanin Gate, a Mamluk style gate with a stone niche at the base of a dome. Israeli soldiers stand at its forest green door, controlling access.

I fish for my *kafiyee* in my backpack, tie it under my chin to cover my hair and approach the entrance where a middle-aged Palestinian man is standing next to Ali's chair.

"Sorry. You aren't allowed," he informs me, politely. "You have to be a Muslim."

"I *am* a Muslim," I reply, defensively.

His eyes tell me he is not convinced.

"Recite the *fatiha*," he orders.

I remain calm, remind myself he is only following protocol, and begin reciting the opening chapter of the Qur'an, trying to be precise when enunciating the Arabic vowels. He interrupts before I finish.

"Go ahead."

He waves me in, handing me a long white skirt. I remove my sandals, pull the skirt over my jeans and enter.

I do not see Amina. Several women are sitting off to the side in a circle, reading the Qur'an in hushed voices. It is serene, even more ornate and sublime than the exterior, painted with mosaics — green, red and white colours against a gold background, floral and geometric patterns, ears of wheat and bunches of grapes. I look up at the vaulted, dome ceiling with its three concentric ambulatories. I pray two *rukaas*, wanting to stay longer, but I know Ali is waiting.

I find him still sitting outside the entrance. "Amina has finished praying and rejoined the group. Can you help me down the steps?" he asks, rising to his feet.

I hold on tightly to his arm above the elbow, and as we slowly descend the stone stairs, I learn he went from terrorist to tour guide. Ali was 17 years old when Israel occupied the Old City in 1967.

"I had to face a new reality, constant beatings and harassment by soldiers and civilians," he says. "I lost my dignity."

As the violence grew, Ali joined the Popular Front for the Liberation of Palestine. He detonated a bomb in West Jerusalem, injuring nine Israeli civilians, and was sentenced to 20 years in an Israeli prison where he taught himself how to speak fluent English, French and Hebrew. In 1985, after serving 17 years, he was released as part of a prisoner exchange between Palestinian and Israeli authorities.

The volunteer olive pickers are sitting on short stools to one side of the Al-Qattinin souk, sipping cold drinks. This stone-arched alley used to be the cotton market. One of the vendors is selling my favourite drink, freshly squeezed pomegranate juice. I buy some for Ali and take a seat near him. He is in the middle of a conversation with some of the olive pickers.

"I live in a prison. I've been a prisoner most of my life," he says, puffing on his cigarette. "The media is one-sided. I want my clients to appreciate what life is really like for Palestinians. As an alternative tour guide, I can educate foreigners. You will see with your own eyes, Palestinian homes that have been stolen by Jewish immigrants."

We finish our drinks. Ali and his assistant lead us through the Muslim Quarter, the biggest and oldest area in the Old City. It is a maze of open air markets and narrow, twisting stone-covered streets, some with steps, smoothed and polished by centuries of foot traffic.

"I want to show you Israel's new Western Wall," Ali says, walking north, away from the Qattanin Market.

I had not heard of the new Western Wall and immediately think of what this means for Palestinians living near it. Bab Al-Hadid Road, a dim, narrow alley, leads to another west-facing entrance to the Noble Sanctuary, the Al-Hadid Gate. Standing guard is an Israeli policeman in a blue uniform talking on his mobile phone, and a soldier in green army clothes. We take a side street near the gate. We cannot go far because it has been barricaded with boxes made of steel bars that are stacked from the ground to the arched ceiling.

"Palestinians living in this area are no longer allowed here," Ali tells us.

I gaze at an ancient stone wall to my right. Like the Western Wall, it has folded pieces of paper in the cracks between the stones, *kvitlachs*. A solitary Jewish woman stands facing it. Her brown hair is pulled back into a bun and she is wearing an ankle-length brown skirt and grey sweater. She holds the Torah in her right hand close to her face, moving her mouth, reciting silently. She does not stop praying to check out the commotion behind her.

I hear the clicking of camera shutters around me. Like many of the olive pickers, I take photographs of her, slightly ashamed of myself for not showing any reverence, yet wanting to document the taking of the Old City, street by street and house by house.

We continue west along Bab Al-Hadid Road to Al-Wad Street, witnessing scattered illegal Jewish enclaves in the Muslim Quarter. Jewish immigrants from around the world have laid claim to these Palestinian homes, as if they exist on some uninhabited moonscape. These homes are easy to spot because of the Israeli flags and surveillance cameras attached to their exteriors, or mounted on rooftops and above doorways. Palestinians are being squeezed out of the Old City, seemingly as easily as the vendor who squeezes pomegranates for a living.

A blue-grey pigeon is perched on a niche above the doorway of a Palestinian home. It stares down at us with orange eyes. As I admire the band of feathers around its neck, glistening purple and green, I hear Amina say to the pigeon, "Go, little one. You're free."

As we carry on walking, I watch the locals, Jews and Palestinians, pass each other without touching or speaking. They do not seem to see each other, even though they likely cross paths every day.

As-Silsileh Street separates the Jewish and Muslim Quarters, where we wander east, passing the fronts of small Palestinian shops. I savour the blaring taped Arabic music, the "Welcome, Madam" uttered by shopkeepers trying to entice me to buy their souvenirs, the open sacks of spices beside vendors' stalls, the men pushing carts brimming with melons and eggplant, and the cornucopia of smells: aromatic cardamom coffee and frankincense smoke wafting through the souk.

As-Silsileh Street ends at another gate by the same name, located along the west side of the Noble Sanctuary, where there is a military checkpoint. Modern steel beams and bullet-proof glass cubicles separate the entrance to and exit from the gate and scanning equipment abut the stone walls and ceiling of the street. We bypass the checkpoint and walk along an inclined street, passing Ohel Yitzchak Synagogue and Khalidi Library.

A husky Jewish man with a grey scraggly beard appears out of nowhere and aims his camera at Amina and me. He makes me uneasy, and I immediately raise my hand to cover my face. I can still sense his dark eyes burrowing through my back as we walk away and turn the corner to an open stone courtyard between some buildings. About thirty Jewish boys are playing in smaller groups. They appear to be around 10 years old. All wear *kippas* and sport crew cuts and side locks. Kiwi attracts their attention with her stuffed kiwi bird. Some of us photograph the boys as we walk through their play area. By now, most of us are accustomed to encountering Palestinian children and know many of them enjoy having their photograph taken.

Within seconds, one boy throws a punch at Amina, who steps back avoiding the blow. A different boy kicks her ankles and yanks her *hijab* from behind. She remains calm and stands firm, facing him. A vein running down the boy's forehead bulges. Spit flies out of his mouth as he yells "Rooh," the Arabic word for "go." Meanwhile, the adults chaperoning the children pretend we do not exist.

Before long the incident is reported to one of the many police officers and soldiers stationed in the Old City. As we ascend to higher ground overlooking the Western Wall, Ali's assistant, Farah, is stopped by two beefy Israeli soldiers.

"Your ID," one of them demands. The other leans into Farah, whispers something and they leave. Farah is stone-faced. The incident has rattled the group. Later, still shaken, he tells me what the soldier said: "When we see you are alone, we will come for you."

The Jewish Quarter feels and looks much different than the Muslim Quarter. Muslim residents pay the same taxes as the Jewish residents, but there is a disparity in municipal services. Jewish homes and buildings are more modern looking, with cleaner streets, parks and green spaces. We pass a newer two-story with a sign that reads:

AISH HATORAH WORLD CENTER:
THE DAN FAMILY OF CANADA BUILDING

Another newer one, fronted by stained glass windows, has a small sign of a hand pointing a gun at the observer and the caption:

FORGET ABOUT THE DOG. BEWARE OF OWNER.

We pass art galleries and souvenir shops, the Burnt House Museum, Quarter Café and Burger Bar. I stop at a small shop to photograph the racks of t-shirts, a proud display of the Israeli narrative, the words and graphics on the t-shirts speak of attitudes and beliefs:

THE BEER CHOSEN PEOPLE CHOOSE
ISRAELI DEFENCE FORCES INTELLIGENCE:
MY JOB IS SO SECRET; I DON'T EVEN KNOW WHAT I'M DOING.

About a block away from an all-girl's play area, there is a sign attached to a building wall, pointing out the way to Bonei Hahoma Road. Like most, the sign is written in three languages: Hebrew, Arabic and English. The Arabic writing is scraped off and replaced with Hebrew words.

"No Arabs. No Bombs," Ali translates for us.

Eventually, the group ends up back in the Muslim Quarter near the Khawajat Market. The bells of a nearby church chime 11 times. It is busier here, livelier than the Jewish Quarter, but it is also unsettling to witness the taking of the Palestinian parts of the Old City by apparently wealthy Jewish people from around the world and the building of homes above parts of the market. The open streets are covered in places with metal mesh to catch garbage Jewish settlers throw down at Palestinians.

I meet several Jewish women who speak English and discover they are from such places as Miami, Boston and New York City.

"I've lived here for the past eight years. My parents live here too, a block away," one tells me, smiling. "It's nice here. Very nice."

I want to say, "You're right. It is nice. Nice for you, but not nice if you are Palestinian."

I stifle the thought. Instead, I tell them to have a good day.

As it often turns out here, plans can change instantly. In the crowded market, Ali slumps down on a chair outside a Palestinian shop, sweating, looking tired and troubled.

"We are behind schedule," Kristel announces. "We do not have time to visit the African Quarter."

As we head west towards the Christian Quarter for lunch, I worry about the incident with the Jewish boys, that our well-intended actions might hurt Farah. I am also disappointed I did not see the African Quarter, but promise myself to come back, hopefully, before it too, is *Judaized*, unlawfully appropriated and populated by Jewish colonizers.

SIXTEEN

Stolen Dreams in Nahhalin

They would open the bathroom door and urinate on us. Our clothes became very wet. From the time of our arrest and for four days, we were tied, blindfolded and detained in confined places without food or water. I was very thirsty, so I had to drink directly from the toilet...I remember that when we were detained in the bathroom, border police would open the door and take pictures of us, or with us. They took pictures of us with our clothes wet with urine to humiliate us and break us down.

M.O., 14 years old, Geva Binyamin settlement, occupied West Bank, "In their own words: A report on the situation facing Palestinian children detained in the Israeli military court system", January 2011

The narrow, sloping street outside the office of the Alternative Tourism Group in Beit Sahour bustles with activity. I stand on the adjacent sidewalk watching Palestinian host families pull up and drop off the olive pickers two or three at a time. Locals, on their way to work, drive by, as do yellow buses loaded with shiny-faced children going to school. The bells of the Lutheran church across the street chime eight times. As I wait for all the volunteer olive pickers to arrive, I sense that this will not be just another day of olive picking. I'm aware of how happy and alive I feel being here.

Today, a full day of olive picking is planned in the Palestinian village of Nahhalin. From Beit Sahour, we drive westerly through a series of higher hills and deeper *wadis*, barren, rocky slopes that have been tamed and made fertile. What still survives of the biblical "land of milk and honey," what has not yet been usurped for settlements, roads and separation walls, is beautiful. Resilient, yet ethereal. I marvel at the stone terraces built by hand using boulders that once lay buried deep in the earth's bowels. Strategic in their location and design, the stone terraces hug the contours of hills and *wadis*, creating unique patterns, anchoring the slopes and transforming them green with olive groves. In the distance, they look like rows of broccoli sprigs poking out of the rust-coloured earth.

Like many Palestinian villages and cities in the Occupied Palestinian Territories, Nahhalin, with a population of more than 6,000, is completely encircled by the Wall. Like many Palestinian villages and cities, Nahhalin has become an enclave, swallowed up by Jewish-only settlements — fortified mini-cities: Betar Illit to the northwest, Neve Daniel to the southeast, Rosh Zurim to the south and Gavaot, which also has a military base, to the southwest. There used to be three roads in and out of Nahhalin. Israel closed two of them.

The bus driver drops us off on a plateau at the edge of the residential area of the village. The autumn air is dry. A layer of dust covers everything. Children loiter in narrow streets littered with garbage.

We lug our bags and olive picking paraphernalia and walk down a gravel path. There are more than 50 of us today. Ten Palestinian students from Denmark have joined our group for the day, and a father and his teenage son from Germany. I sense eyes watching us as we descend into a narrow valley. I look up. At the top of the ridge facing me is the Bitar Illit settlement where about 30,000 Jewish people live. We *are* being watched. My eyes follow a road built exclusively for Jewish people further down the slope leading to the settlement. Running parallel to the road is the Wall, an electrified metal barrier topped with razor wire. A military watchtower stands next to the Wall. Anxiousness creeps in. I have the same nervous feeling everywhere I go in the Occupied Palestinian Territories.

Waleed, a Palestinian farmer, meets us at the edge of an olive grove huddled at the bottom of a narrow valley. He owns over 200 olive and other fruit trees on three separate, non-contiguous parcels directly beneath Bitar Illit settlement. The olive pickers split up. About half the group stays behind to pick olives in the first parcel. I walk south with the rest about 100 metres. Led by Waleed, we follow a path in the red earth along the valley bottom, passing more groves of olive and grape and copses of peach, plum and cactus pear, separated by stout, stone fences running east to west up the slope and serving as property boundaries.

Waleed's second parcel stretches up a terraced slope. Everyone begins laying tarps under the olive trees, and we get to work, "milking" the olive branches the way we were shown on the first day.

I pick a spot near Waleed and strike up a conversation with him while we harvest. I learn that the settlement looming directly above us is partially built on land that his family has owned for more than 100 years. Israel seized this land forcefully without notice or compensation, ironically after the Oslo peace talks of 1993.

"Jewish settlers and soldiers often prevent me from accessing the 50 *dunams* (12 acres) that remain of my land," he says. "I am afraid. I know what is left can also be taken at any time to expand the settlement."

Nahhalin's water resources are also being usurped for settler use, creating a water shortage for village residents. The sewage plant in Bitar Illit cannot cope with the settlement's growing population.

"The excess waste is often discharged into the valley towards Nahhalin," Waleed tells me. "The settlers have contaminated our natural springs and crops, and caused diseases in the village."

About an hour later, as I'm taking a break to drink and jot down some notes in the shade of an apricot tree, Waleed's teenage nephew walks over and says hello. When he realizes I speak Arabic, he sits beside me on a low, stone fence.

"Are you a journalist?" he asks.

I shake my head. "I'm working on a book about my experiences here."

He's 18, the youngest of four boys in his family. He looks like a typical Canadian teenager in his blue jeans and t-shirt. He is soft-spoken. His big brown eyes stand out, and there's a sadness to them that pulls at my heart.

"I was in an Israeli prison for 14 months. I recently got out," he says, eager to talk about his experience.

"It would be my privilege if you shared your story," I tell him. "I won't use your real name."

"They accused me of throwing stones at Israeli soldiers," he starts.

"Did you?" I ask, out of curiosity.

"No. I wasn't even interested in politics. All I cared about was school. I wanted to study medicine and become a doctor. They came for me at two in the morning. It was November 19, 2008. Soldiers, many of them, busted into our house, yelling my name. They grabbed my parents and brothers and forced them outside. One soldier yanked me out of bed, demanding to see my ID. They shackled and blindfolded me and threw me outside, dragging me across the ground like an animal. They pushed me into a military jeep and told my parents they would bring me right back and drove off. I thought I'd never come back home."

He stops talking and looks down. "I'll never forget my mother screaming and pleading with the soldiers to let me go," he says.

Thankfully, his mobile phone rings. I don't want him to see me crying, hating that I cannot control the tears. He apologizes and takes the call. Sitting next to him, I can't help but overhear. It's his mother, checking to make sure he's all right. He tells her he's fine, "*Alhamdulillah*," and that he's just chatting with one of the volunteer olive pickers, a Lebanese lady from Canada.

He is only a few years younger than my son. I can't imagine how his mother felt, her helplessness. I don't know what I would do or how I would fight back if my teenage son was suddenly snatched in the middle of the night.

Waleed's nephew's case is not unique, but commonplace. According to the 2011 Defence for Children International – Palestine Section report to the United Nations' Special Rapporteur, each year about "700 Palestinian children as young as 12 years of age are arrested, interrogated and prosecuted in the Israeli military court system. Credible reports of ill-treatment and torture within the system are common and persistent." Of the 645 complaints filed against Israeli prison authorities from 2001 to 2010, not one investigation was conducted. Israeli soldiers continue to abuse Palestinian boys with impunity.

He finishes his call and slides the phone back into his pocket.

"I didn't know where they were taking me," he continues his story for me. "I was wearing only pyjamas. It was cold. My wrists were bleeding because the plastic shackles were squeezed too tight. They took me to a compound where I was interrogated and beaten. I told them I never threw stones at Israeli soldiers. I never once thought of throwing stones at anyone. One of the soldiers recorded my statement in Hebrew. I didn't have much to say, a few sentences, but the statement he later wanted me to sign was pages long. I wouldn't sign it, so they beat me and threatened to arrest my older brother, who was about to travel to Jordan to get married, if I didn't admit to throwing stones. I refused to admit to something I didn't do. They beat me some more.

"After two months of interrogation I was taken to a prison in the Negev. It was close to a cattle farm. The smell was unbearable. The prison had eight large tents surrounded by a 12-metre-high, electrified fence. Each tent had 22 prisoners. Beds were stacked above each other. We were treated worse than animals. Winter nights in the Negev are cold. We were often shackled in contorted positions for long periods, often deprived of food."

As I listen and take notes, I visualize him being tortured, tied up, his joints aching and limbs numb, hungry and afraid.

"Sometimes, they put worms and cockroaches in our food. Or they would put something in our food to keep us awake. Or something to put us to sleep. I never knew what I was eating exactly or what I was drinking. I got a bad skin infection and allergies," he says.

He lifts up his shirt to show me his pitted and scarred back.

The Israeli authorities gave him old clothes to wear that had mould growing on them. He was never allowed to see a doctor. They locked him for long periods in a cement box measuring one metre by two metres. They would move him to a new tent whenever he developed a bond with another prisoner. He saw his parents only once during the 14 months.

"Others had it much worse. You could cry for them," he says, looking at me with eyes wiser than his years. "Some were serving life sentences, old men. Some died there without their families even knowing of their whereabouts.

And there were boys younger than me. Israel prefers 12- and 13-year-olds. They scare easier. There was sexual abuse. The older prisoners took care of me."

He goes quiet.

"Tell me about the day you were released."

"I couldn't believe at first," he says. "A month before, one of the guards asked me if I wanted anything. I told him, 'I want my stolen childhood.' He wrote my answer down, surprised. It wasn't a happy day. Israel let me out of prison. But I'm still not free. I'm still a prisoner. I can't travel. I'm not even allowed to be here on our land. I went from a small prison to a big prison. Freedom is not granted. You have to get it yourself."

I learn that he loves poetry; he recites a couplet from a poem he likes. I understand only part of its meaning, something about a "bridge of hope built over a river of despair."

"I kept a diary while I was in prison," he tells me. "I called it, 'Tha'ir Inside Prison.' The guards took it away from me the day I was released. But it's still in my head. They can take it all, but they can't take my memories. It helps to talk about it, even though it hurts."

"What are your plans for the future?" I ask.

"I learned knowledge is my weapon. I wanted to be a doctor, but I can't now," he replies.

He missed two years of school and decided instead to become an engineer. His father's income cannot be stretched further to pay for his university tuition, but his father promised he would beg on the streets if needed to pay for his schooling."

"I would like you to pick a pseudonym for yourself that I can use."

"Call me Safi. I love that name," he says, "It means 'clear' or 'pure.'"

Just before lunch, our group is picking olives on a terrace higher up the slope, close to the electrified metal barrier protecting the bypass road leading to the settlement. An army jeep approaches and stops. Six soldiers, dressed as if they are heading to a war zone, march down the road towards us, looking ready to spray us with bullets. Gravel crunches beneath their boots. At the same time, directly across on the opposite hillside, another army jeep emerges and stops. My heart sinks. I know the Israeli soldiers have the power to do whatever they want.

"What are you doing here?" one of the soldiers yells. "Who are these people?"

"Volunteers. They are helping me pick my olive trees," Waleed answers calmly. "We are almost done."

"You must leave the area immediately," the soldier orders, swatting at the air with his hand, shooing us away.

We quickly gather our things and walk further south along a trail at the bottom of the valley to another olive grove. Clumps of cactus pear grow between the rocks on either side of the trail. The rest of the olive pickers soon join us and Waleed's sons and nephews bring lunch: several steel pots, charred black on the bottom and edges, filled with steaming *maqlouba*. We sit in the shade of the olive trees, eating and listening to one of the Palestinian students from Denmark share her group's experience yesterday in Silwan, a Palestinian neighbourhood in East Jerusalem, where Israel plans to demolish numerous Palestinian homes to make way for a Jewish settlement and theme park. One of the girls does the talking. Obviously still traumatized, tears stream down her cheeks as she describes their visit to the International Solidarity Center in Silwan.

"We heard bombs and shooting as a convoy of army jeeps descended into the neighbourhood. We saw four soldiers snatch a Palestinian boy off the street near his home. His friends and other children began throwing stones at an army jeep. The soldiers fired back at them with tear gas and live ammunition.

"We were all crying," she says, trembling as she relives the experience. "A boy came up to us and told us not to be afraid, trying to be a hero. He was only 10. He had already been arrested and detained five times — for 'terrorism.' He showed us his scars where he was shot by Israel soldiers."

This is a fact of life lately for children in Silwan and elsewhere in occupied Palestine. They are taken away from their homes and punished just because they are Palestinian. Some of them are brought back, many are not.

Like Safi, an olive tree picked before his time, it is the same story for most of the families I meet in the "Holy Land." A story of teenagers yanked from their beds in the middle of the night, tortured and imprisoned without reason or due process. Of teenagers denied an education and medical help, deprived of their basic human rights. A story of stolen dreams, dashed possibilities and lost innocence. Of teenagers surviving immense humiliation and pain, still they remain hopeful and aspire to become doctors, teachers and engineers.

Waleed comes up to me and says, "I would like to say a few words to the group. Please, would you translate for me?"

"I'll do my best," I reply. I was not expecting to be put on the spot. Several of the olive pickers record us. He speaks quickly and with passion.

"Thank you for coming here. Your help means a lot to me. Without your presence, I likely would have been prevented from picking my olive trees. In the past, I have been attacked by settlers and I have even been jailed by the Israeli army for trying to tend to my fruit trees.

"As you can see, we are not the terrorists," he says, looking around at the group. "As you can see, there is no peace on the ground, only talk, propaganda. Meanwhile, Israel continues to take more of our land and to rob our children of their dreams and destinies."

I maintain contact with Safi after returning home, always happy to hear he was staying strong, hopeful and encouraged by his eagerness to finish high school and start university. On December 31, 2010, hope was replaced with dread. I receive a short e-mail from Safi's friend, saying: *I'm sorry to tell you Safi has been arrested by the Israeli army again. He's now in prison. We don't know where they have taken him.*

SEVENTEEN

The Wild West in Palestine

Nonviolent resistance is everywhere. Children wait for hours at checkpoints on the way to and from school every day because they are determined to get an education despite the obstacles; Palestinians and Israelis camp out together as partners for peace in spite of widespread attempts to turn the war into one of Jews versus Muslims; a movement leader returns from prison after 13 years and goes back to the nonviolent resistance he was arrested for; an old woman, armed with only her voice and determination, confronts a bulldozer uprooting her trees and the fourth strongest military protecting it; a shepherd grazes her sheep despite the threats of poison and settler attacks...Palestinians are not strangers to nonviolent resistance; they are champions of it.

Anna Baltzer, Witness in Palestine:
A Jewish American Woman in the Occupied Territories, *2007*

It's Friday, October 22, 2010, the Muslim holy day, and at sunset it will also turn into the Jewish Sabbath. Friday is also a free day for the international olive pickers. The night before, the olive harvest organizers had taken a poll during our debriefing. Some of the olive pickers decided to visit Jericho and the Dead Sea, while others wanted to explore the Bethlehem area. My head nagged me to play it safe and visit Jericho and the Dead Sea, but my heart pulled me to Bil'in.

In the end, my heart won and now 22 of us are on our way to participate in a weekly, non-violent protest against Israel's confiscation of Palestinian lands, and building of the Wall and settlements in Bil'in. I had read that these demonstrations have been taking place every Friday since February of 2005.

Friday has become a day of non-violent demonstrations in many villages and cities all over occupied Palestine.

By nine in the morning, our convoy of three yellow vans is weaving through Bethlehem. Our driver, Nidal, a tall Palestinian with hazel eyes and an acne-scarred complexion, leads the way. I am sitting in the front seat next to him.

The landscape abruptly changes as we ascend through a series of stony, sun-baked mountains, mainly white with splashes of light brown. From the top of one mountain, I see the road below winding its way along the base of two ridges, an undulating black ribbon, stark against the pale terrain. We reach the Container checkpoint; the road is not blocked. We do not have to stop, although there is a military watchtower nearby. An Israeli settlement dominates the top of a high ridge, blotting the beauty of the rural landscape. We pass road signs indicating access to Jerusalem, Hadassah Hospital and Mount Scopus. The driver concentrates on the road. The others in the van watch the passing landscape in silence.

I take photographs of the Wall running parallel to the road, trying to suppress the anger growing inside of me. Israel's settlement policies and practices, its empty promises of peace, its continued military occupation are clearly visible on the landscape. I see the proof everywhere I travel, but still cannot believe it, cannot accept. It saddens me to witness. The highest ridges in the Palestinian territories continue to be stolen from Palestinians, their peaks shaved down, built-up and occupied by Jewish people from many parts of the world. I cannot help thinking, "It is a 'free for all' if you are Jewish, a modern-day Wild West. Where is the condemnation from global leaders?"

"Does anyone notice what is happening here?" Nidal interrupts my thoughts, speaking as if to himself, eyes glued to the road.

"Does anyone care? Who's going to stop Israel?"

I do not respond. I do not know what to say.

At the bottom of a wide valley, we drive past what looks like a rivulet. The sinuous, narrow fringe of green vegetation along its banks grabs my attention. I twist my neck back, stare at it until we round a bend and it disappears from view.

"It is not natural," Nidal tells me. "It is sewage from the settlement above."

We continue through an arid expanse of beige and rust-coloured hills. Here and there are clusters of Bedouin tents on either side of the road and small herds of sheep. We come to another checkpoint. Nidal stops and shows his ID to a soldier, who waves us through. He pulls the van to the side of the road and waits.

"The limit is seven passengers. The van behind us has eight," he explains, while peering into the rear-view mirror. Luckily, the soldier does not object to the extra passenger or perhaps he does not notice, and allows everyone to cross the road barrier.

Nidal puts the van back into gear, and we head west, where the landscape becomes greener. Grape orchards and olive groves grow in neat rows on terraced slopes. I'm not certain where we are exactly, only the general direction we are travelling. Nidal is also unsure.

"I have never been to Bil'in before," he admits at one point. "None of us have."

I am not worried. I tell myself that he'll eventually find the tiny but defiant village. It has received global attention, yet it seems too few people back home know about it.

"I'm afraid to make a wrong turn and end up in a settlement," he confesses. His fear is real. He stops countless times along the way to ask, "Which way to Bil'in?"

"It's ahead," with a finger pointing the way, is the reply.

It helps to know we are still headed in the right direction. Several times, when no one is stopped along the road for him to ask, Nidal honks the horn at the driver ahead of us, who knows the road code, and eventually stops or slows down so he can ask, "Which way to Bil'in?"

"Continue on this road for another half hour."

It's almost 11 in the morning when we reach Bil'in. We pile out of the vans near the village mosque, where demonstrators typically gather. Several

Palestinian teenagers approach us, selling key chains and beaded bracelets. One of them is wearing a red t-shirt. When he notices me clutching a camera, he turns around, proud to display the caption on his back:

DROP KNOWLEDGE, NOT BOMBS.

We head over for a briefing at the nearby headquarters of the International Solidarity Movement in Bil'in. The sidewalk leading to the stone office building is lined with manicured shrubs. A young pomelo tree, bearing four large yellow orbs, grabs my attention. Ahead of me, a cloth banner titled, POPULAR STRUGGLE OF COORDINATION COMMITTEE is draped on the outside wall above the doorway to the new office building, where we enter. The banner displays the photographs of committee members and their names.

We file into a meeting room on the first floor. Its walls are covered with posters. Photographs of bloodied people being helped. Soldiers man-handling an elderly Palestinian woman. An uprooted olive tree lies on the ground next to two men who are looking up at a settlement on an adjacent hill. I notice some of the people in the group crowded around one poster. It is titled:

APARTHEID: WRONG FOR SOUTH AFRICANS,

WRONG FOR PALESTINIANS

Underneath, are two side-by-side photographs. One, taken in Soweto, South Africa in 1976, is a black and white image of a man running with an injured boy in his arms. The other, taken in 2004 in Gaza, Palestine, captures a similar scene in colour, of a man, whose mouth is open in anguish as he is carrying his injured son.

"Welcome, everyone," a tall middle-aged Palestinian man says in a loud voice. The group quiets. The man is wearing brown-tinted glasses and holding a poster that says:

FREE ABDALLAH ABU RAHMAN

"My name is Ali. Thank you for coming," he says. "I will start by giving you an overview of Bil'in's non-violent resistance movement."

Bil'in is a small village of about 1,800 Palestinians. Israel usurped 2,800 *dunams* (692 acres) of the 4,000 *dunams* (988 acres) of Palestinian-owned land to build the Wall and settlements.

"We refuse to relinquish our rights," he says in a calm voice. "We refuse to be silenced about the theft of our agricultural lands and the destruction of our olive groves.

"Residents of Bil'in began holding peaceful demonstrations on February 20, 2005. We have held non-violent demonstrations every Friday since then. We often use various creative methods of resistance.

"Earlier this year, several demonstrators dressed up like the movie characters in James Cameron's *Avatar*, who, as you know, also fought against exploitation and domination."

I imagine the demonstrators painted blue, donning pointed ears and long tails, and wish I could have been here to witness the reaction of the Israeli soldiers, who would have been waiting for them.

Did they crack a smile upon seeing them? Were they amused? Did the demonstrators make them think? Did they even care?

"Once, during the construction of the Wall, we chained ourselves to olive trees to prevent them from being uprooted," Ali continues. "The media came. Israeli human rights activists and international activists came. Jimmy Carter and Desmond Tutu were recently here."

He pauses and looks around at the olive pickers.

"From the beginning until now, people like you from around the world have come to join in the demonstrations in Bil'in. The week of Israeli's murderous raid on the flotilla carrying desperately needed aid to Gaza, the people of Bil'in lifted the same 32 flags raised by activists on board the ships."

The Popular Committee Against the Wall in Bil'in has won some small battles. In 2007, the committee petitioned the courts for restitution. The Israeli Supreme Court ordered the military to push back the Wall. In Israel, though, the military reigns supreme. They continued their illegal settlement building, changed the route of the old wall, an electrified fence dangerous to both humans and wildlife, and built a new section of wall consisting of side-by-side concrete slabs over eight metres in height.

Israel also installed a gate in the Wall. Residents of Bil'in now need permission every time they want to access their land on the other side of the barrier, which hinges on the whim of the soldier and is seldom granted. The Israeli army still refuses to comply fully with the court order. It has given back only some of the land to their rightful owners.

Ali does not mention that the struggle in Bil'in is also being fought in Canadian courts, which I hoped he would have. I learned that on October 2, 2010, less than two weeks before I came here, residents of Bil'in filed an application before the Supreme Court of Canada, suing Green Park International and Green Mount International. Both are Quebec-based companies, who have been "involved in the construction, marketing and selling of residential units in the illegal Israeli settlement of Modi'in Illit," which is built on confiscated Palestinian land in the occupied village of Bil'in. Canada's highest court subsequently dismissed the application for leave to appeal on March 3, 2011.

"The Israeli army continues to oppose any peaceful resistance by imprisoning, injuring and even killing protestors," he continues. "The people of Bil'in and other demonstrators, including internationals, pay for speaking out.

"More than 1,300 demonstrators have been injured. Some even killed. Most of the residents of Bil'in have been arrested at some point. Children have emotional disorders from all the violence."

He stops and props the poster he was holding up against the meeting room wall.

"After the noonday prayers, we will walk to the wall. Don't be afraid," he says. "Don't taunt the soldiers. The army will shoot at you with tear gas and sound bombs — sometimes real bullets."

I have never heard of sound bombs and wonder if they are intended to break eardrums or disorient or both.

"Your eyes will burn badly, but whatever you do, DON'T RUB THEM," Ali warns.

If others in the group are afraid, they do not show it. Some, like Marcos and Alicia, a couple from Spain, have come prepared.

"We brought extra," Alicia tells me, slips the backpack off her shoulder and pulls out the baggie of quartered onions stashed inside.

—❧—

The soothing call to prayer from the nearby mosque drowns out the din of the growing crowd of locals and other international protestors. Everyone is relaxed it seems, except me. I try to push aside worries of all the terrible things that could happen. My family comes to mind. I am grateful they are not here to see me in this setting. They would worry.

I start up a conversation with several young activists from Israel. One of them, Talia, is a beautiful girl with curly hair and long lashes that accentuate her sparkly green eyes. She is wearing a t-shirt with ANARCHISTS AGAINST THE WALL written across the front.

"Have you demonstrated in Bil'in before?" I ask her.

"Yes, many times." She smiles.

"Do the soldiers *always* shoot tear gas?"

"Always," she replies. Sensing my fear, she rummages in her backpack. Here. It's my last one." She hands me a small sealed antiseptic wipe. "It will trick your mind. Open it and sniff it when they shoot the tear gas."

I want to learn more about her, but the demonstration begins.

Internationals shout, "FREE FREE PALESTINE," over and over. I'm near the front of the procession, beside Amina, who is waving a Palestinian flag, and Sophie, who is holding a poster of a man Israel has imprisoned for demonstrating. Several of the demonstrators are clutching a banner that says, in English:

WE WILL STAY HERE LIKE THE ROOT

OF THE OLIVE TREES.

The noise builds as we make our way through the streets of Bil'in. The air is electric. Local boys and men march with flags or posters of activists arrested by Israel, singing and clapping, smiling at the international demonstrators. The atmosphere is jubilant. I do not get it. I forget my fear and join in as the demonstrators shout slogans in Arabic: condemning Israel's military occupation, the siege on Gaza, the ethnic cleansing of Palestinians in East Jerusalem. I feel privileged. I have a profound sense that I was meant to be here. It was my destiny. Many of the internationals stop at the sides of the street to take photographs. We pass a camera crew and reporters. The procession lengthens as more locals, including children, join the flanks ahead of me, cheering and clapping. Within five minutes, I am near the back of the demonstrators. By now, we number about 100.

We reach the outskirts of Bil'in, a high point with a panoramic view of the adjacent hills and the Wall marring the pastoral scene. The demonstrators, now quiet, continue west on the narrow, paved path, which dips down a slope, bisecting an olive orchard before rising up the adjacent hill. I lag behind, taking photographs of used tear gas canisters that litter the ground. Colin, a nine-year-old activist from England, spots them first. A typical curious boy, he bends down for a closer look.

"Don't touch them," his mother, Jeni, who is standing at his side, cautions.

I am surprised to see so young an international demonstrator and even more surprised that his mother would bring him to such a protest given the inherent dangers. And I am intrigued.

What motivated him to come to the occupied territories? Is he fearful?

I ask his mother these questions.

"He wanted to help the Palestinians with the olive harvest," she explains. "He is not afraid of much."

I want to ask other questions, but I realize they are not going any further than the outskirts of Bil'in, and I've put some distance between me and the back of the procession, now more than 100 metres ahead. I take photographs of the backs of the demonstrators. Those at the front have crossed through the olive grove further down the slope and are following the narrow path as it rises up the adjacent hill towards the Wall. As I zoom in with my telephoto lens, it takes me a few seconds to believe my eyes. Leading the demonstrators is a man in a motorized wheelchair, manoeuvring around the rocks on the path. My shock turns to amazement at his courage, which I do not fully grasp. I am flooded with different thoughts.

Are the soldiers actually going to shoot at an unarmed, disabled Palestinian who is demonstrating peacefully? A proverbial sitting duck? Because they have the power? How will he be able to move out of harm's way?

I worry, too, about Amina, who is walking right behind him, fearlessly waving a Palestinian flag. She is only 19, yet we have become friends. I am fond of her, and the mother in me feels a constant need to protect her.

I photograph the occupying army waiting for us at the top of a hill. The scene through my small-town-Alberta eyes is scary, even from a distance. Nine soldiers stand like Rambos near the gate in the Wall, dressed in full military gear, armed with machine guns and tear gas launchers, fully protected behind an electrified, four-metre-high fence topped with coils of barbed wiring.

As I gawk at them through my viewfinder, I wonder what their orders are for today.

Shoot to scare? Shoot to injure and maim? Shoot to kill? I wonder also, *who is willing to stop them?*

Here, the Israeli army is the law, and it matters little if the demonstrator is a foreign national. My heart pounds against my rib cage. I notice the unusually cloudy sky and feel cowardly for intentionally lagging behind. Perhaps it's not a matter of courage or cowardice, rather my motherly duty to my children. I want to show solidarity with the Palestinians, raise my voice against Israel's military occupation, but I also want to live to inform others.

Something in me takes over after seeing the disabled demonstrator. I want to be there with him. I hurry to catch up and merge into the middle of the group.

Suddenly, the Israeli soldiers start shooting. A series of loud popping sounds sends those near me running in the opposite direction. I glance back at a barrage of black projectiles flying towards us, hissing and sputtering, releasing white curls of smoke. I pull the front of my shirt over my nose while I run and hold my breath as long as I can. The mountainsides are quickly enveloped by a toxic white haze. I am forced to breathe the air, forced to stop running. My eyes burn and tear. My throat and nose are on fire. I remember the antiseptic wipe from Talia in my pant pocket. I dig it out, tear it open and sniff it, but it does not help.

The soldiers fire more rounds of tear gas. Everyone around me is hurting, sputtering and coughing. Marcos, from Spain, hands me a piece of onion. I sniff it, but combined with the tear gas, it makes my stomach turn. A couple of men hold a boy upright, who looks about seven and is having problems breathing. They lay him down under a tree and tend to him. Another young boy sits on the path with his head between his knees because he can't see.

Several people vomit. I wonder about the health of Bil'in residents who are continually exposed to the tear gas.

There are more loud pops and sputtering. I look to the sky, trying to predict where the tear gas canisters will land. Some fall close by. A young Palestinian man picks up an oozing canister and throws it away from the demonstrators. Another man kicks at one canister.

We are being shot at with tear gas from two directions. Beyond the olive grove, further up a slope to the north, is another group of soldiers firing at us from behind an east-west segment of the Wall.

A couple of small fires erupt in the dry grass under the olive trees. Several teenagers beat at the flames with branches and stomp them out before they spread. I retreat from the olive grove to higher ground to photograph the demonstrators at the front, focusing on the young man in the wheelchair. His back is to the soldiers and he, too, is taking photographs of the mayhem. I am relieved to see he is wearing a gas mask. Fifteen minutes later, he and the others at the front slowly make their way back through the olive grove.

Several local teenagers stay behind and start throwing stones at the soldiers. It is as if I am watching a re-enactment of David and Goliath. Two of the Palestinian teenagers use slings, but none of the stones even come close to hitting the metal barrier, let alone harm the soldiers who shoot back with more tear gas. For a brief moment, I am disappointed. This was supposed to be a non-violent protest, but how can I expect these teenagers to practice non-violence when they are being attacked by armed soldiers simply for resisting Israel's occupation and the confiscation of their lands?

The stone throwing and tear gas launches continue for about half an hour as internationals watch and take photographs. I think of how my own three children might react if they lived in Bil'in. I see traces of my son in one of the teenagers, and imagine him throwing stones despite my pleas to stop. Eventually, the soldiers end their tear gas assault, perhaps out of boredom, and people make their way back to the village less than a kilometre away.

The man in the wheelchair is still snapping photographs. I notice his professional Nikon camera and that he is using only one hand, the other one rests lifelessly at his side. I walk over and introduce myself. His name is Rani, a 30-year-old who lives in Bil'in.

"Weren't you scared being right up at the front"? I ask, after exchanging pleasantries, thinking to myself, "How can you *not* be?"

"No. I've been shot at many times," he answers nonchalantly. "They even shot at my wheelchair."

He looks me in the eye and says, "Giving up is scarier. Not resisting the Occupation is scarier. If we don't stand up for our rights and our freedom, Israel will take what it hasn't already. It will take all our land."

He pauses.

"Were you afraid?" he asks me with a slight smirk, head cocked to one side, squinting into the sun.

"I was terrified," I answer. "I have demonstrated several times before back home in Edmonton, but city police did not shoot at us with tear gas and sound bombs."

Rani pulls down the neckline of his shirt, exposing a scar on his throat and tells me, "It wasn't a regular bullet, but the expanding type. It cut an artery and came out my back. It ripped through my internal organs and severed my spinal cord."

Rani was shot on the first day of the Second Intifada, September 30, 2000. Three days earlier, Prime Minister Ariel Sharon and hundreds of his soldiers stormed into the Al-Aqsa Mosque as people prayed. Demonstrations broke out across the Palestinian territories. Rani was part of a group protesting at a checkpoint near Ramallah. The Israeli army responded to the peaceful protest with live ammunition. Rani and many others were shot. His condition was critical. From a hospital in Ramallah he was taken to Amman, Jordan, for further medical treatment. He was hospitalized for seven months.

"Imagine my father hearing on the radio that I had died," he says. "I was in a coma for months and I had many operations, but with God's help I pulled through."

"*Alhamdulillah.* You made it," I tell him.

"*Alhamdulillah.*"

"Nice camera. I see you like photography too," I say to him as we continue up the road.

"I have taken thousands of photographs and hours of video of the demonstrations. Once, I recorded my younger brother getting shot in the thigh by soldiers."

I would love to see his collection of photographs, and think about the power of images to communicate and inform. The idea of organizing a photo exhibition of Rani's work in Canada pops into my head.

We reach the outskirts of Bil'in. Rani stops and points to a stone house about 50 metres away. "That's my house. It is typically the first one the Israeli soldiers raid at night," he tells me. "They often fire tear gas and live ammunition into it. Three family members have been wounded."

I learn that Rani used to dream of completing school, becoming an electronic engineer. "All I want is to live a normal life. I'm married now. I have three baby girls! Triplets," his eyes light up, matching his wide smile. "I just want to raise my girls and live in peace. Israel deprived me of an education, but I'm hoping my daughters will become engineers."

"*Insha'Allah*," I say, expecting to say good-bye now.

"It would be my honour if you come to my house for a cup of tea," he offers.

"The honour would be mine. Thank you," I say, pleased with the opportunity to spend more time with him.

Amina and Sophie, who were walking alongside me, join us, after I spot our driver and ask him to wait a bit longer. We follow Rani to his house, a modest bungalow style. A cement ramp leads up to the front door. He introduces us to his wife, who greets us at the door holding one of the triplets, and to his father who is busy in the kitchen. Rani leads us out a sliding glass door to a stone patio in the backyard. Seated around a long table are several Israeli activists, including Talia, a man from Japan, and several locals. It dawns on me that this gathering might be a regular Friday ritual following every demonstration.

In a few minutes, we are treated to typical Arab hospitality. Rani's father brings out a large pot of sweetened mint tea and small glasses, followed by three big platters of *hummus*, plates of olives and *labnee*, and a basket filled with warm pita bread. I'm still nauseous and have no appetite, but Rani and his father insist I eat. They remind me of my parents, who do not take "no," for an answer when it comes to food. Not wanting to offend them, I tear off a small piece of bread and dip it into one of the plates of *hummus*.

We are only here about half an hour before a local teenager is sent after us. We part ways and head towards the mosque, where our drivers and the rest of the olive pickers are waiting. As our convoy heads back east towards Ramallah, Rani consumes my thoughts.

Today, I met a true hero. Israel stole his family's land, stole his chance at an education, stole his limbs, his inherent human rights, but it did not defeat him or diminish his dream of freedom, of one day living in peace. I have no doubt, for as long as Israel continues its occupation and colonization of Palestine, Rani will be there every Friday to resist, peacefully leading the demonstrators with camera in hand, documenting soldier violence, facing the odds. Knowing that he could be shot again, aware that he might not return home alive to his wife and baby daughters, but he will remain undeterred and unafraid.

EIGHTEEN

Maintaining *Sumud* in the Shadow of an Outpost

To Alef, the letter
That begins the alphabets
Of both Arabic and Hebrew –
Two Semitic languages,
Sisters for centuries.

May we find the language
That takes us
To the only home there is –
One another's hearts.

Alef knows
That a thread
Of a story
Stitches together
A wound.

Ibtisam Barakat
Tasting the Sky: A Palestinian Childhood, *2007*

"Outpost."
The Oxford dictionary defines this word as, "a small military camp at a distance from the main army," and as "a remote part of the country or empire." For me, the word reminds me of the black and white Hollywood westerns I used to watch on television, conjures scenes of the Wild West in North America centuries ago, a thing of the past. But, in

the Occupied Palestinian Territories, outposts are very much a thing of the present. Built on the highest ridges, Israeli outposts are ubiquitous on the landscape; that is how many Jewish settlements start out. A few trailers and an Israeli flag appear overnight on a hilltop, and in a short time grow into gated towns for Jewish settlers. Local Palestinians call them "caravans," which invokes for me images of a circus coming to town for a few days, something temporary and benign. I find the word an unintended euphemism because in occupied Palestine, outposts are precursors to illegal colonies.

Today, I am picking olives at the base of one of these outposts near the Palestinian village of Al-Khader, about five kilometres away from the western outskirts of Bethlehem. The olive orchard belongs to Sumud (I name him this because the Arabic word means "steadfastness") and his brother Muhammad. Jewish colonizers recently seized more than half of their land for the outpost. They subsist on money generated by their olive orchard and by growing a variety of vegetables in a rust-coloured field on the valley floor. The remaining land, 38 *dunams* (over nine acres), is at risk of being stolen to expand the new colony.

We are watched over by three rows of white trailers on the slope above us. We have been picking since nine this morning near a high, wire fence, presumably built to protect the outpost. The fence truncates a piece of Sumud's land and prevents him from accessing the olive trees on the other side, which extend higher up the slope.

I pick mechanically, sensing someone is watching. Not knowing what might happen next is unsettling. This feeling stays with me like a shadow wherever I go in the Occupied Palestinian Territories. It is not an exaggeration to say our group is likely being watched most of the time by settlers or soldiers. It is not about being paranoid or pessimistic. It is neither impossibility nor improbability. At any moment, one of the armed settlers living in the white trailers perched above me might become enraged by our "siding" with the Palestinians. I believe that my presence and participation in the olive harvest makes me a target for settler and soldier violence, especially because I am an Arab. Here, every place I visit, I am reminded of my *Arabness*, and of being the *other*. The fact that many Palestinians and Israelis I encounter mistake me for being Jewish and address me in Hebrew does not ease my fears.

At one point, I look up at the outpost. A tall man dressed in black pants and a white shirt stands outside one of the trailers, looking in our direction. Half of his face is hidden in the shadow of a hat he is wearing. I continue picking, curious to know where he came from. In the Old City of Jerusalem, I encountered Jewish people who moved there from the United States, Canada, Russia and Europe. I wonder if he feels any remorse for illegally occupying private Palestinian land.

Does he feel any guilt for swindling Sumud of his destiny? Does he even consider the impact of his actions on Sumud's young children?

I remind myself that a significant number of Jews believe God gave them this land.

Who am I to argue with God?

Israel has the power, the resolve and the backing and blessings of many world leaders.

After picking for about an hour, I stop for a drink of water and notice two of the Korean women standing next to Sumud. Maria is holding a microphone near his mouth and Solby is videotaping. I walk over. Sumud is trembling, wiping away tears. Solby lowers her camera. It is clear the interview is over. He shakes his head as if to dislodge a painful memory and quickly pulls himself together.

"The settlers living in the trailers do not harass me," he says, changing the subject. "Not like the ones living in the settlement of Neve Daniel."

He points to the nearby ridge. I am surprised to hear that some of the settlers in the outpost are friendly towards him.

He chuckles. "They often ask me for snippets of sage."

I learn later from Maria why Sumud was upset. "He witnessed Israeli soldiers shoot his mother and brother." She cries as she tells me this.

Later, everyone crowds around one of the tarps where the Korean women have made a peace sign out of olives. Solby, the youngest in the delegation, asks us to sit around it with our arms out-stretched. The atmosphere is filled with laughter and the chatter of friends. It is heart-warming to witness the creativity of the Korean women, their wish to acknowledge the olive branch as the eternal symbol of peace. Wanting to capture the moment, we hold still, smiling. Shutters click and cameras are passed from person to person to the top of the human circle and into the hands of a willing photographer.

My stomach gurgles. I check my watch. Three hours have passed.

"Finish bagging the picked olives and gather your things," Baha, one of the olive harvest organizers, announces in a slightly elevated voice.

Sumud looks to me and Leila, one of three, young Moroccan activists from the Netherlands. She is standing beside me with her backpack slung over one shoulder.

"Follow me," Sumud says without explanation, pointing to an olive orchard further up the slope.

He grabs one of the black plastic buckets and leads the way up a path beside a stone fence. He's spry and familiar with every boulder and hollow. His gait is long and effortless. I guess him to be in his early fifties, like me. It doesn't take long before Leila and I are out of breath as we struggle to keep up. I sense urgency in Sumud's steps. He looks back often, wide-eyed, making sure we are still behind him, and glances around as if expecting someone to show up.

Sumud suddenly stops in the middle of an olive grove. I look around me. It feels magical to be standing in the dappled light, surrounded by stately olive trees, admiring their root-like branches and knobby trunks. A blanket of dust covers their slender grey-green leaves and their clusters of olives the size of small plums. I have not seen this variety before and marvel at the profusion of blue-black colour and perfectly round shapes hanging elegantly.

Olive trees have been cultivated in the Mediterranean region for over 10,000 years. Generations of my family grew olive trees on their land in Lebanon. Olive oil is revered and described as "green gold." Ambrosial. Edible and delicious. Medicinal. And, like the indigenous peoples of the Holy Land, both Arab and Jew, the olive tree is resilient, managing to grow in impoverished soils, protruding at extraordinary angles from the rocky, steep slopes. These trees, too, have endured for millennia, clinging to the dry, sun-wizened earth, longing for peace.

"You can pick from any tree. Just fill the bucket. Hurry," Sumud pleads.

I see him from the corner of my eye as he moves frantically from one tree to the next, and glance at him as his fingers gently pull the fruit free from the branches. I want to understand exactly why he is so nervous and not assume, but I do not ask. It soon becomes clear when we hear a vehicle. Sumud stops picking. The three of us look up the slope in the direction of the sound. There is a road, which I cannot see, but soon taste as a cloud of dust descends on us. The vehicle continues without stopping. False alarm.

Sumud's shoulders drop and we resume picking. In no time, we have filled the gallon-sized pail plus a couple of plastic bags, which Sumud has stashed in his pants pocket, and we head back down the hill.

We walk across a vegetable field at the valley bottom. Sumud's teenage nephews are planting rows of cauliflower saplings. Leila wants to help them, so we stop for a while. Sumud and I wait in silence. I gaze at the outpost to the north. It breaks my heart to know that in no time the outpost will mushroom into a settlement for Jewish immigrants, and this rich, bountiful earth will be lost. As the song goes, "They paved paradise and put up a parking lot."

We rejoin the rest of our group outside a solitary stone house shaded by a variety of fruit trees. I find a spot to sit under a mature fig tree and dig into my bag for my pen and notepad. Off to one side of the yard, about 20 metres away, Sumud is praying. After prostrating twice, he sits up, with his legs tucked back. His head is bent slightly and he is bathed in white light. I'm moved. I have no doubt he gives thanks to God for what he has, and wonder what, if anything, he asks of Him. I jot down some notes and, when I look up, I see he has finished praying. He walks over to where I am sitting, carrying a generous sprig of lemon verbena. He tears off a leaf, rolls it back and forth in his fingers, releasing an aromatic mixture of lemon and mint, and drops it into my outstretched hand.

I inhale its fragrance. "It's one of my favourites," I say. "Every year, I try growing lemon verbena, but with little success."

He sits cross-legged on the ground next to me. I sense he has something on his mind. "I don't want you to think I left you out. I know you did not get to hear my story," he says apologetically, gesturing at the notepad.

"No worries. I didn't think that. Maria told me what happened. I don't want you to re-live that day."

"I re-live that day, every day," he replies. "I think about my mother and brother every day. It was at the start of the Second Intifada in 2000. The Israeli army placed the village under daily curfews and regularly conducted night raids."

He goes silent for a few seconds.

"They killed them for no reason and barred the ambulance from coming to our home," he resumes in a calm voice. "No one was allowed to leave their homes. We could not bury them for two days."

"*Asfee*." I say. I'm sorry is all I can manage to tell him as I struggle to imagine the unimaginable.

The olive pickers form a line on the stone patio next to Sumud's house and fill their plates from the array of food laid out on a long table: lentil soup, stuffed zucchini, stuffed grape leaves with the traditional yogurt on the side.

Sumud's voice rises above the chatter.

"Help yourselves. Help yourselves to seconds." I scoop some lentil soup into my bowl and take a seat.

After I finish eating, I get to talk with Sumud's sister-in-law.

She tells me, "My mother was killed during the Intifada. They would not let me see her."

She tears up and starts rocking herself. "Forgive me," she says, "but it is not easy to forget. She was shot over forty times."

I am tongue-tied, numbed. It is only when I hear Baha say, "Time to go. Our bus is waiting for us," that I realize I, too, am rocking in my seat.

Sumud and Muhammad drive ahead of the group, taking a couple of the olive pickers with them. Our bus driver is not allowed to use the side road to Sumud's house. I say my goodbyes to their families and walk with the group about 300 metres towards the highway where the bus is waiting. An Israeli army jeep is blocking the end of the side road. A second army jeep is parked near the highway. Four soldiers march straight towards Baha.

"Your ID," one of them demands.

Baha fishes in his backpack and hands it over.

"What kind of protest is this?" the soldier asks him, irritably. As Baha explains, I aim my camera at the soldiers. Before I can snap a photograph, Albert, one of the olive pickers from the Netherlands, taps me gently on the shoulder from behind and shakes his head. It angers me to witness this control and humiliation, angry enough to turn around and snap several photographs after they let us go. I do not care. The olive pickers begin boarding our waiting bus.

Before I do the same, Sumud says, "I'll give you my telephone number."

I hand him my notepad.

"You are always welcome in my home," he says as he writes his number down.

I feel a lump in my throat and turn my face away.

"Don't cry," he tells me, shaking my hand firmly.

Tenderness radiates from his eyes. "*Khaleekee salbee,*" he says. "Stay strong."

Tears burst from my eyes against my will. I feel sheepish and selfish. Relatively speaking, I have nothing to cry about. I am not the one dispossessed of my land and deprived of family members. I am not the one living without my freedom in the shadow of an outpost. Instead of comforting Sumud, he is the one who remains steadfast and consoling.

NINETEEN

A *Dabke* Flash Mob for the Occupier at Wad Ahmad Checkpoint

God is the Light of the heavens and the earth. The parable of His Light is as a niche in which there is a lamp; the lamp is in a glass; the glass is as if it were a glittering star, lit from a blessed tree, an olive, neither eastern nor western, whose oil would almost illuminate although no fire touched it. Light upon Light. God guides to His Light whom He will.

Chapter 24:35, Holy Qur'an
Translated by Laleh Bakhtiar, The Sublime Quran, *2007*

We have been waiting in our bus for over an hour. It's early Sunday morning, the last day of the olive harvest campaign. As usual, we are stuck at a checkpoint on the northern limits of Bethlehem. Israeli soldiers have closed the metal gate in the Wall. Nothing is moving. We have been in this position before during the past two weeks, every time we wanted to leave and return to Bethlehem.

I should be accustomed to all the controls on freedom of movement, and having to cross checkpoints. Frustration sets in. I fidget in my seat, thinking how Israel's military occupation has become entrenched, normal for Palestinians; nothing appears more carved in stone. How can they make any long-term plans for their lives when routine, daily activities are burdened with obstacles and doubt? They never know if they will get to their destination, if they will be allowed to cross the myriad Israeli checkpoints blocking their path, if they will be harassed, delayed or even if they will return home safe. For Palestinians in the Occupied Palestinian Territories, travelling a few kilometres to go to school or work, or to visit their family or doctor, is a journey of uncertainty that can take several hours each way.

Kristel is talking on her mobile phone with Ajmal, the landowner, to let him know about our delay. I hear her discuss an alternate, albeit longer, route to Wad Ahmad, where we will be picking olives. The grove is located near a monastery along the slopes of a picturesque valley outside the village of Beit Jala. There are two access points to the 90 *dunams* (22 acres), which Ajmal's family has owned since the late 1800s. Not only did Israel confiscate some of his land, they also built a gate across the gravel road at one of two entrances, the shorter of the routes leading to his home from the highway. The Israeli army issued Ajmal the only key to the gate, ordered no duplicates be made and barred non-family members from using the road. They also prohibited the use of all types of automobiles on the road, forcing the family to walk or drive a scooter from the connecting highway.

After finishing her call to Ajmal, Kristel tells us, "Ajmal had, in advance, asked the Israeli commander in charge for permission for our group to cross through the gate. The commander refused and warned Ajmal that if he opens the gate for us, he will have big problems."

The commander also threatened to cut off water and electricity to Ajmal's house. Kristel explains that without our help he will not be able to pick his olives before they spoil.

"We have no choice but to access Wad Ahmad from the opposite side. Ajmal may still face problems if we use this alternate road. At least he can say he did not break the rules," she says, grinning.

The gate for vehicle traffic at the checkpoint finally opens.

"No photographs. Don't say anything," Kristel warns as we inch forward. "Remember, you're peaceful pilgrims."

The bus driver stops. Two armed soldiers board our bus.

"Passports," they demand as they amble down the aisle.

One at a time, we surrender them. When it is my turn, I hand mine over to a barely-adult-looking soldier brandishing an M16. He gives it a cursory look, gives it back to me and directs his attention to Martha, the elderly activist from England, who is sitting across the aisle from me. She rummages through her bag.

"I'm afraid I've forgotten it in Beit Sahour where I'm staying," she says weakly to the soldier. Flustered, her face glows bright crimson, contrasting a head of snow-white hair. She offers the soldier her British health care card, hand trembling. To my surprise, and likely hers too, the soldier accepts it as proof of identification. They make their way to the back of the bus, where Amina likes to sit. At least this time she is not being singled out. Or so I think.

She calmly hands her passport to one of the soldiers. He takes his time, scrutinizing it more closely, making sure she has not exceeded her two-week visa.

"Yes, I know it expires tomorrow," she tells him, smiling. "Don't worry. One more day and you'll be rid of me."

The soldier returns her passport without responding. They leave through the side door and the mammoth steel gate in the Wall opens.

About half an hour later, the bus stops on the side of a highway. Thirty metres ahead, a checkpoint that we do not have to cross straddles the road. Soldiers standing sentry watch as we jaywalk across the highway with ladders and buckets in hand. We head west on a gravel road built about halfway up the mountainside; it curves to the left and we are surrounded by pine-covered slopes. I notice that I no longer hear the hum of the vehicles on the highway, immediately feel the calmness of this tiny verdant oasis. So far, this spot has been spared from the rush of encroaching Israeli settlements. It is not until I look back in the direction we came from that I see a settlement dominating the top of a ridge, which I could not see when we were dropped off. Further down the slope is a brown complex, a petting zoo, which I assume exists exclusively for Jewish people.

The road rises gradually. A gentle breeze laps against my face. The stillness is punctuated only by the occasional banter of the olive pickers and the scraping of shoes on loose gravel. I spot a deer across the narrow, steep valley and stop to watch as it scales its way up terraced slopes dotted with olive trees, and disappears into the pines higher up. I can't help but feel sad wondering how long this patch of dwindling habitat and tranquility will last before it is stolen from its owner and stripped away for another Jewish settlement.

After walking for about a kilometre, we meet up with Ajmal, who is waiting for us on the side of the road. His short black hair is jelled back and he is wearing stylish jeans and a pink polo shirt.

"Thank you for coming," he says. A smile lights his dark, handsome face.

He points to a terrace of olive trees further down the slope where we need to go and we descend slowly, zigzagging in a line. I avoid stepping on loose rocks and brushing against the knee-high clumps of dry thistle that are ready to poke through my pants and pierce my skin. I am more worried about encountering a snake sunning itself, but manage to push aside the thought when we reach the row of olive trees. A blue tarp has already been laid beneath one of them.

"Please. Do not include any leaves," Ajmal instructs us. "And do not start on another tree until every olive has been picked."

We set to work. Amina and Solbe climb up the tree and assume their usual spot in the higher branches. Today, I want to stand on firm ground and pick the olives within my reach, listening to the plopping sounds as they hit the tarp where others are ready to gather them into steel buckets. Ajmal continues in the background with his "dos and don'ts."

"Be careful. Please do not to break the branches," he pleads, still smiling. "These trees are like family. We even have names for them."

I think to myself, "If this tree were mine, I'd name it 'Husin,' after my mother, my biggest hero." Her name means "beauty" and "good manners" in Arabic. She has both attributes.

Refreshments soon arrive by scooter. It is Ajmal's older brother bringing pots of sage tea and a basket of warm home-baked spice cookies, which I recognize as *kaak*. My mother, my grandmothers and their grandmothers before them have, for centuries if not millennia, made a similar type of Arabic cookie.

The aroma takes me back to my childhood in Lac La Biche, Alberta, where

I grew up. Coming home from school on a bitter winter day, I remember being greeted at the door by the aroma of freshly baked *kaak*, a bouquet of cloves, cumin, cinnamon, and *mahleb*, a nutty-flavoured spice made from the ground up seed kernels of a black cherry tree.

As we rest, I have the opportunity to learn more about Ajmal. Like me, he has ties to South America. "My great-grandfather immigrated to Chile in the 1920s," he says. "Ten years later, he returned to Palestine."

Ajmal also spent several years living in Chile. He is a Christian Palestinian in his early thirties, a charismatic bachelor who speaks multiple languages and works as a tour guide.

Feeling comfortable enough, I ask Ajmal, "Do you want to get married one day?"

"I would like to, but how can I save enough money to get married?" he replies, without self-pity. "The Israelis often cut the electrical cables and water to my house. Each time I end up paying thousands of shekels to restore service. Money I don't have."

He looks me in the eye and calmly asks, "What would I tell my children? There is the wall. This is our land. That is our boundary. Why would I bring children into to a life of subjugation and discrimination?"

Abu Khalid, an elderly man who owns land in this valley, shows up suddenly for a visit. He kisses Amjad on the cheeks and extends his hand out to me.

"I saw you yesterday at the olive press in Bethlehem," he tells me, smiling.

"A pleasure to meet you," I shake his hand. I do not remember seeing him.

He sits on the edge of the tarp, wanting nothing more, it seems, than to pass some time chatting with someone from another country. I sit down beside him.

"I can tell by your accent, you're Lebanese, right?" he asks.

I nod my head. "*Muzboot.*"

His tanned face is lined like a contour map, yet his honey-coloured eyes sparkle with youthful vitality. He shares that he once visited Beirut when he was younger.

"God forgive them. They destroyed it. It used to be the 'Paris of the Middle East,'" he laments, shaking his head.

After drinking a small glass of sweetened tea, he slowly gets to his feet. Ajmal and I stand up to say good-bye to him.

"God be with you," he says, gripping my hand.

He no sooner turned his back to leave when we hear a sharp *CRACK*.

In seconds, John, an olive picker from France, drops to the ground from one of the branches where he sat picking. He quickly gets up and brushes himself off. A flushed complexion betrays his embarrassment. Thankfully, he did not injure himself. Meanwhile, Sophie, who was sitting on the tarp almost directly under the fallen branch, is holding her blonde head between her knees. Ajmal immediately rushes over and empties his water bottle over her head, asking over and over, "Are you okay?"

She raises a dazed face streaked with tears and nods.

"Are you sure?" He gently parts her hair. "No blood. It's only a small welt," he says, loud enough for the group."

Everyone is relieved.

Dusty and tired, but in high spirits at having the chance to help Ajmal pick his olive trees, we climb back up the slope to the gravel road. It is only a five-minute walk to his home. The modest stone-covered dwelling is perched above the road, fronted by a terraced slope and cement steps leading to a veranda shaded by two orange and blue umbrellas. Several trees beside the house are laden with olives. Bright pink bougainvillea spills over a stone terrace.

Ajmal's widowed mother, Maria, greets us, beaming. She is middle-set, attractive with high cheekbones and almond-shaped eyes. Maria and Ajmal fuss over us, pouring cold drinks and dishing out copious amounts of *koosa*, zucchini stuffed with savoury rice and cooked in a tomato broth. We enjoy our lunch outside on the veranda overlooking the valley. It is the same generosity and hospitality I have experienced with every Palestinian family I have met.

With Ajmal translating for her, Maria apologizes for not having more umbrellas. "We bought a sunroof, but the Israeli army would not let us put it up. 'No improvements,'" she explains.

She points to the mountaintop directly across from us. I had noticed the communications tower nestled in the pines and the surveillance equipment mounted near its top.

"They watch us constantly," Maria says in exasperation.

After lunch, she invites us inside her rustic cabin-like home. The interior walls are also stone-covered. Maria's embroidery work, which she sells to help sustain her family, hangs from pegs in the walls and lay in neat stacks on end tables and the only sofa. Knowing it will help her out, some of the olive pickers buy a variety of embroidered bags, wall hangings and wallets.

Later, we congregate outside. Many of us take photographs of each other. Maria pulls me aside.

"I would like to say a few words to your group, but Ajmal has disappeared somewhere on his scooter. Would you please translate for me?"

"It would be my pleasure," I say.

The olive pickers gather around her on the patio. I listen, translating her words to myself and recording the English rendition in my notepad. She pauses intermittently to give me time to convey her message by reading back what I have written.

"You cannot imagine how happy I am to see you here, to know you care about us," she says looking around at us. "From my heart, I thank all of you for your help." She stops. Her smile vanishes.

"Israeli soldiers barred us from using a car to get to and from our house. We are forced to carry our necessities about two kilometres to our house," she says.

"I miss my family."

Her voice cracks. She blinks back tears.

"They are not allowed to use the road. So no one comes to visit. If we get sick, the Israeli soldiers will not allow anyone in to help us. Our life here is harsh. But, we won't leave our land."

She shakes her head, pauses. "It takes *sabar*, patience. After *sabar* there is *faraj*, relief," she says with conviction in her tone, as if to herself.

I am reminded of a similar expression that my mother often uses:
Al sabar muftah al faraj. Patience is the key to relief.

"Tell them. Tell the people in your country about us and how we live."

It is late in the afternoon when we arrive back at the end of the gravel road leading to Ajmal's house, at the main highway where we were dropped off earlier this morning. Some of us flop ourselves on the ground at the side of the road near the checkpoint to wait for our bus. Ajmal, who came along, waits with us. Kristel is on her mobile again.

"Our bus driver is stuck at a checkpoint," she informs us after hanging up.

I glance around at the group to find that no one appears surprised or bothered. Such delays have become normal for the olive pickers, too. We pass the time taking group photographs. Suddenly, Kristel walks to the middle of the road and begins dancing, smiling widely, gyrating and shaking her hips like Shakira to an imaginary beat. We gather around, clapping and cheering her on. I admire that she spends months in the Occupied Palestinian Territories every year, working for the Alternative Tourism Group during the olive harvest and tree planting campaigns. She is becoming more fluent in Arabic and is familiar with the local traditions and culture, mastering several Palestinian dance styles.

Ajmal joins her on the impromptu dance floor. Others start dancing, too. The air is electrified with mirth and innocent fun. Laila shares music on her iPhone. Nancy Ajram, a Lebanese pop star, sings her latest song. Albert, who is off to the side of the dancers, starts doing the twist as we chant his name.

"ALBERT. ALBERT."

The clapping intensifies as others join in, kicking up tiny dust clouds, dancing "as if no one is watching."

Meanwhile, the soldiers at the checkpoint stare back at us. I wonder what the soldiers are thinking. Two of them are close enough to where I am standing at the edge of the gravel road, that I can see their expressionless faces.

They do not look amused. At first, I am shy to join the dancers. I remain in same the spot, moving my hips only slightly. I am nervous.

What if one of those soldiers is in a bad mood? What if he is angry about something, angry enough to think we are mocking him, and God forbid, he loses it and starts shooting at us?

With all the fun the olive pickers are having, dancing, laughing and clapping, it is easy to dismiss my fatalistic thoughts. My alter ego surfaces. I wrap a *kafiyee*, around my hips, tying it on one side and join the dancers on the road, carefree, with youth-like abandon. The olive pickers erupt in loud cheers, whistles and shouts of approval.

At one point, Sabah plays her iPhone. Michael Jackson sings "The Way You Make Me Feel." It is a surreal moment, 40 peace activists from around the world, dancing to the King of Pop in the occupied Holy Land.

"I have an idea!" Kristel yells out. "Let's have a flash mob for the soldiers. We can do the *dabke*."

Her excitement is contagious. I am very familiar with the *dabke* — literally, the word means "stamping the feet." It is a traditional Arabic folk dance, a line dance, which my father forced me to learn when we attended Lebanese weddings. No matter how hard I tried to stay off his radar, he always managed to spot me in the crowd of attendees and gently tug me by the arm against my will to the dance floor. Deep down, I enjoyed it, once I got past my insecurities and shyness.

"I can teach you guys," Kristel encourages. "Come on. It will confuse the soldiers at the checkpoint."

She laughs mischievously.

We all know Kristel has organized flash mobs in the Netherlands, her home country. There is no resistance from the group. We join hands, forming a human string behind her and imitate her movements as she demonstrates the steps. Before long, everyone gets the hang of it: two steps, a slight hop and a stomp. We move as one, back and forth on the road, a human chain stepping and stomping to the beat I still hear in my head, my father playing the *durbuke*, a small Arabic hand-drum that is shaped like an hourglass and often used as a solo instrument for *dabke* and belly dancers.

Tuk Tuk Dom. Over and over. *Tuk Tuk Dom.*

That beat feels as if it has been hard-wired in me. Before live bands and DJs came into vogue at weddings, my father happily provided the entertainment for free — literally a one-man show. At the time, he was the only Lebanese in Lac La Biche, who could play the *durbuke*, and he had a wonderfully soulful singing voice, entranced his audience with love ballads and *mejana*. He would be the last to leave the hall, beating the *durbuke* late into the night, fingers swollen, sweating, but content.

The *dabke* stops, but the volunteer olive pickers carry on, clapping and cheering. The soldiers continue gaping, standing slackly, weapons hanging from their necks. They know we are foreigners and leave us alone. I am curious if the soldiers appreciate our peaceful message: we are dancing for fun and freedom, and to oppose their pervasive presence in the lives of the Palestinian people living in the Holy Land.

I could never have predicted this moment, participating in my first flash mob, which one of the olive pickers records and later posts on *YouTube*. I stand on the dirt road, grateful our bus was delayed, gaze at the olive pickers, their clothes oil-stained and coated by reddish dust. The late afternoon sun casts its golden glow; their smiling faces glisten with satisfaction.

TWENTY

Democracy in Sheikh Jarrah: Israeli Style

There is on the horizon of the Middle East a new awakening; it is growing and expanding; it is reaching and engulfing all sensitive, intelligent souls; it is penetrating and gaining the sympathy of noble hearts. The Middle East, today, has two masters. One is deciding, ordering, being obeyed; but he is at the point of death. But the other one is silent in his conformity to law and order, calmly awaiting justice; he is a powerful giant who knows his own strength, confident in his existence and a believer in his destiny

Kahlil Gibran, "The New Frontier," 1943

In Jerusalem, I meet up with Paulo and David as planned at the Educational Bookshop on Salah Eddin St. Hoping to avoid extra interrogation at the airport tomorrow, Paulo and David hand over their books and Palestinian memorabilia to the shop owner and begin filling out forms to have the parcels mailed to their home addresses.

I have been thinking for days about the "pro-Palestinian" books I am taking back home. Mailing them to my home address would be cost prohibitive. As I wait for Paulo and David, I rationalize that the books are replaceable if they are confiscated. I am more concerned about my camera's memory cards containing thousands of photographs, two notebooks of research notes and a personal journal, all of which is irrefutable, detailed proof of my "activities."

I am more than a benevolent tourist. I am a Palestinian sympathizer.

When it is my turn, I place my memory cards on the counter.

"Could you please burn my photographs to a DVD?"

The shop owner nods, picks them up and drops them into a small envelope.

It annoys me to have to pay 80 shekels ($22 Canadian), but I do not want to risk having my documentation commandeered and destroyed by airport security officials. Or worse.

"I'll come back later in the day to mail some other items home," I say to him over my shoulder on our way out.

It is almost noon. We buy some Mediterranean-style chicken wraps at a fast food place nearby and eat as we walk to the Az Zahra Hotel, where we meet up with more peace activists from England: Ian, 20-something, Jina and her 10-year-old son, Colin. I met them all for the first time last Friday at the demonstration in Bil'in. We are going to spend our last day in the Holy Land by revisiting the Jerusalem neighbourhood of Sheikh Jarrah.

It's a 10-minute walk to Sheikh Jarrah. We follow Nablus Road north, passing the Tomb of the Kings and the American Colony Hotel. On Othman Ibn Affan Street, we turn east and stop in front of Rifqa Al-Kurd's yard. Maysa, Rifqa's middle-aged daughter, is at the gate leading into their yard just like she was two weeks ago when we first visited.

"*Ahlan*," she says, smiling as she kisses Jina and me on the cheeks, and shakes hands with the men in our group.

Eric, a 70-something activist from England is already here, standing next to a dingy solidarity tent set up to one side of the Al-Kurd yard. Through Paulo, I learn that Eric, nicknamed Abu Mahmoud by the Palestinians, has Syrian and Jewish roots. He kept a one-man-vigil for more than four months last year, sleeping in this spot to protect the Al-Kurd family from harassment by Israeli settlers, soldiers and police. For his peaceful resistance, Israeli soldiers shot him with rubber-coated, steel bullets and arrested him. He is a quiet, elderly man, with a small stature, and he tends to glance around furtively.

I feel the tension in the air. I do not wish to be an imposition and worry that our presence might make the situation worse for the Al-Kurd family.

I ask Maysa, "Did we come at a bad time?"

"*La la, habibti,*" she assures me warmly and welcomes us into her yard. Before going in I take photographs of the Hanoun home across the street, which is now occupied by several Jewish families. That is when I notice a Palestinian woman standing motionless in front of the two-story complex.

"Her name is Mariam," Maysa tells us. "Israel forced her family from their home in 2009, all four generations, 38 members, 12 of them children — one born the night they were evicted."

I find it difficult to imagine what she has endured. My heart goes out to her.

How much can a person suffer?

She walks over to us. Her blue eyes betray an intense sadness, but she smiles politely as we introduce ourselves.

"I come here every day," she tells me when she hears me speak Arabic. "It's a stab in the heart to look at my home from the outside and not be able to go in.

"I planted that orange tree," she says wistfully, pointing to the tree in front of her seized home. A row of Israeli flags hangs across the top of the two-story complex. They flutter freely in the slight breeze.

We step inside the sit-in tent. I take a seat on a worn sofa and record her words as she describes how they were evicted, stopping her every so often so I can translate her ordeal to the others.

"It was like a war," she begins. "Israeli soldiers, commandoes, surrounded and closed down the entire neighbourhood. It was February 2, 2009. We were all sleeping. At 4:45 in the morning, I woke up to a very loud sound. Israeli soldiers had blown open the front door with explosives. All of them were dressed in black. They quickly filled our home, grabbing the children first and throwing them into the street as if they were little birds. They beat us. I tried to shield my nine-year-old son. They took my sick father-in-law, an 88-year-old man, and pushed him out the door without his wheelchair. He died 10 days later of a heart attack."

Her voice cracks. She pauses for a few seconds, rocking and staring at the ground in front of her. Tears run down her face. She quickly brushes them away, takes a deep breath and goes on.

"I was forced outside in my night clothes, without my hijab. Barefoot. A neighbour gave me a blanket for cover. My son kept asking, over and over, 'Where is our front door? Where is our front door?'

"They tossed our furniture out on the street. Trucks came and they began moving the settlers in, taking some of our furniture back inside. It took them less than an hour to seize our home. We stood outside as dawn broke. Terrorized. For hours, my son quivered as if he was being electrocuted. He is still traumatized and cannot fall asleep without me at his side."

I wonder how many times Mariam has told her story to the many activists like us who come to participate in the sit-in. I worry about the emotional cost of retelling her story, of having to relive the horrors of that night.

"Where does your extended family live now?" David asks me to ask her.

"They are split up and living with other relatives," she explains. "For the first six months after we were evicted, we camped out in front of our house during the day under a fig tree beside the street.

"We had no place to relieve ourselves, no wood to make a fire for cooking, no warmth at night. The UN offered us a tent, but the settlers kept stealing the rocks that we used to pin it down. Israeli police fined us and confiscated our tent 17 times."

They spent the month of Ramadan, fasting while living on the street. At night, Mariam slept at Rifqa Al-Kurd's house. Now, she rents a one-bedroom apartment a few blocks away for her family of six, and relies on her older children's pay checks to cover their expenses.

"Israel took everything. I've been imprisoned twice," she says, "but, even if they cut off my oxygen, I will not leave."

Emotionally worn-out, her face is flushed.

"Thank you for listening. Thank you for visiting Sheikh Jarrah," Mariam tells us.

The afternoon sun is fierce and forces us to a shady spot further back in the Al-Kurd yard, between two separate houses. One, belonging to Rifqa's married son, is located near the front of the rectangular lot and is now occupied by several Jewish men. The other home sits at the back of the yard and belongs to the elderly Rifqa. White wisps of hair poke from under the beige scarf tied under her chin. She appears tired and weary. I help her carry over some plastic lawn chairs stacked near a pile of furniture outside her son's house and arrange them in a circle on a stone pad between the two homes.

Jeni, her son Colin and Paulo decide to go to buy some sweets for the family. Soon, several Palestinian women who live in the neighbourhood drop by to visit. We sit together, chatting comfortably as if we have known each other for years. Maysa brings out small cups of Arabic coffee for everyone.

"Who do you think did this to us?" one of the women asks, taking a sip of coffee before answering her own question. "The British. They gave away Palestine, but it was not theirs to give."

Everyone nods in agreement.

"We have God," adds Rifqa, looking up at the cloudless sky with unwavering faith.

"Last week I noticed my flower garden was wilting," Mariam interjects after a brief moment of silence. "I felt sorry for it and couldn't just leave it to die. So I got up on a chair to reach over the fence. As I was watering the flowers, one of the settlers came and kicked the chair from underneath me.

"Israel jailed me three times in the past, just for looking at my house and I had to pay fines. I keep coming back when my children are in school. It's my home. My family built it 54 years ago.

"Once, my nine-year-old son accidentally brushed the mirror of a military jeep as he walked by it," Mariam carries on. "Twenty soldiers attacked us, shooting tear gas, beating us. They took my son. I was too sick from the tear gas to stop them. Later, I went to different hospitals searching for him. Eventually, I found him at a police station, shackled in a small room, still blinded by the tear gas. They kept him in prison for two days without medical help. After we paid a fine, Israel released him."

"When the Jews seized my son's house," Rifqa adds, "my four-year-old granddaughter became sick, feverish and unable to sleep. She was terrified to leave the house. For days, my granddaughter was inconsolable and cried over and over.

"'They took my house. They took my swing. They burned my bed. They put a gun to grandma's chest.'"

I sit in stunned silence for a few seconds, imagining the scene. I write down the little girl's words, now seared into my memory, repeating them to myself, thinking how poetic they sound, a verse from a Palestinian nursery rhyme.

Rifqa explains that her granddaughter was watching as Israeli soldiers threw the child's bed outside and burned it. The soldiers also beat Rifqa unconscious and arrested her. It is difficult to accept that any soldier could do that to a defenceless, old lady. Israel not only took her son's house, forcing him and his family to move in with her and Maysa, but it also issued an eviction order against Rifqa's house, a one-bedroom place where 12 members of her family now live. She is scheduled to appear in court in January 2011 and has resigned herself to being evicted. She has already boxed up some of her clothes and personal belongings.

"I have no one. I have nowhere to go," Rifqa says.

Suddenly, there is a commotion at the front end of the yard. I hear Maysa's raised voice, but cannot make out what she is saying. All of us get up to find out why. She is near the sit-in tent, trying to stand in the way of three Jewish men dressed in similar white shirts and black pants. They have come to resume their shift by occupying her brother's house. My heart races and I pray the situation does not turn into a violent confrontation. Maysa is no match for them. She has been beaten by settlers and soldiers in the past and arrested several times by Israeli police for resisting her brother's displacement.

Two of the men remain silent as they walk past without looking at us and quickly duck inside the house. I sense they are showing restraint, perhaps because we are international witnesses. The third, a teenager, stands near the front gate of the Al-Kurd yard talking on his mobile phone, laughing. He saunters towards me. When he draws close, he points his phone at me to take my photograph. I panic. Without thinking, I push his arm away, immediately realizing I should not have touched him. I scurry back to where we were sitting as he shouts at me in Hebrew. I do not dare look back. Rifqa, Maysa and the other activists also retreat to the rear of the yard. The visiting women disperse.

"It is time to pray. Excuse me," Rifqa says, and heads inside her house.

"Wait and see. They are going to arrest me again," Maysa laments after we sit down. There is fear in her eyes. They are not the brave eyes that gave me strength and inspiration the first time I met her two weeks ago.

The horror stories I heard from some of the human rights activists I met flood back. This terrifies me even more. I begin to worry that my photograph will end up in the hands of Mossad or security officials at Ben Gurion airport in Tel Aviv tomorrow. I worry, too, that Maysa will somehow pay for my actions.

I'm rattled to my core. It took only a few seconds to shatter my shallow bravado, and I'm aware I'd make a terrible resister. I can't imagine living with the constant tension and violence, deprived of my dignity, powerless and without rights and recourse. I'm also filled with admiration and respect for every Palestinian living here. For their courage. For coping with life as the "other," as virtual prisoners. For the dignity they display despite the constant threat of being displaced, the controls and curfews, harassment, imprisonments and beatings. For their patience and perseverance. For turning the other cheek and their continued non-violent resistance. For not running away.

But where would they run to?

Most of the Palestinians currently living in Sheikh Jarrah are already refugees, displaced from their towns and villages in 1948. Many, like Rifqa Al-Kurd, who fled to Sheikh Jarrah from Haifa in 1948, are now being dispossessed once again. Rifqa's family used to own three lucrative businesses in Haifa before Israel drove them out.

"Jimmy Carter was in Sheikh Jarrah yesterday," Mariam mentions casually.

There is a moment of silence. I sense someone watching us and turn to see. The young man who took my photograph is now inside the house at a window overlooking the patio where we are sitting. He starts making lewd gestures and blowing kisses at me. I give him my back, trying to ignore him.

Then I hear the voices of Jeni and Paulo, who have just returned. Grateful for the distraction, I get up and walk to the front gate to meet them. A camera crew has also arrived and is filming a male reporter, who stands in the street with his microphone, his back to what once was the Hanoun family home. Some of us start snapping photographs. The reporter notices us and stops.

"Who are you? What we are doing here?" he asks, looking at each of us.

"I don't want to get shot," he explains in an apologetic voice, without waiting for a reply. His raised shoulders drop when Paulo tells him that we are peace activists who came to help Palestinians harvest their olive trees, but it does little to alleviate his apparent nervousness. He motions for the camera crew to follow him and they leave in a hurry. I assume they were trying to avoid a confrontation with the Jewish settlers and soldiers. I learn only that he works for the UN.

Just when I think our time in Sheikh Jarrah is over, Mariam informs us about a sit-in at the east Jerusalem office of the International Committee of the Red Cross. Three men, elected members of the Palestinian Legislative Council have been seeking refuge at the Red Cross compound since July 1, 2010.

"They have been there for 117 days. Do you want to meet them and hear their stories? It's not far. I could take you there," she offers.

We all jump at the chance. We say our goodbyes to Rifqa and Maysa and the seven of us follow Mariam as she leads us west on Othman Ibn Affan street. We pass orthodox Jews in long black coats and square hats, walking north. Mariam explains that the men are going to pray at a cave known as the Tomb of Shimon Hatz.

"But the man who died in the cave was an Arab. They're actually praying to a dead Arab," she says, almost amused.

I cannot tell if she is serious.

We cross Nablus Road and walk past a small park to our right. Across from it is a run-down crowded area where graffiti litters the walls of houses and doorways. Without speaking, Mariam points to a Palestinian home with an Israeli flag and camera above its doorway. There are cameras mounted on the exterior of all the stolen homes in Sheikh Jarrah, and elsewhere in

Jerusalem. Within five minutes, we have reached the Red Cross compound. A large white banner is draped on the stone fence facing the street. In both Arabic and English, it reads:

WE WILL STAY HERE FOREVER.

A middle-aged English-speaking man greets us at the gate.

"Hello," he says, smiling, as if he expected us. "I'm Omar."

We introduce ourselves. He is used to greeting visitors, who come to meet the men and participate in the sit-ins, and gestures us inside the compound yard.

"The men are having their dinner now," he tells us. "But they would be happy to meet with you right after they finish."

"Thank you. That's not a problem. We can wait for them," Paulo tells him.

I notice the protest tent to one side of the compound yard. A banner at the top of it tallies the number of days the men have been here, 117 DAY FOR THE PLC SIT-IN. More banners, written in Arabic and English, cover the surface of the three-metre cement fence flanking the tent:

JERUSALEM IS AN OCCUPIED CITY.

OCCUPATION MUST LEAVE.

We sit on plastic lawn chairs lining the north and east walls of the compound opposite a stone-faced building. Facing us, on the building's wall, is a large poster superimposed with photographs of four men, elected members of the Palestine Legislative Council. One of them, Deputy Mohammad Abu Teir, stands out because of his bushy red beard and blue eyes, appearing more like a Scotsman than an Arab. Israel arrested him the night before the other three politicians sought sanctuary at the International Committee of the Red Cross. He currently languishes inside a military prison.

In the past, Israel also imprisoned the three men we are waiting to meet: Mohammad Totah, Ahmad Anoun and Khaled Abu Arafeh. For more than four years they were in and out of prison, accused of "disloyalty" to the State of Israel simply because they are elected members of the Change and Reform Party affiliated with Hamas. The Palestinian elections of 2006 were overseen by international observers and deemed fair, but the will of the people has yet to come to fruition. Israel and many countries, including Canada, have labelled Hamas a terrorist organization. Palestinians are trying to practice democracy, but are simultaneously punished for voting for the *wrong* party.

When the men refused to renounce their affiliation with Hamas in the spring of 2009, Israel revoked their ID cards, issued to all Palestinians of east Jerusalem, which permit them to reside in Jerusalem, but do not grant them citizenship. Israel then ordered the politicians to leave Jerusalem by July 1, 2010. I can't help wondering why Israel arrested only Abu Teir. Israeli police and soldiers are more than capable of snatching the other three men at any time.

Why have they not done that yet?

The man who greeted us hands out invitations to future sit-ins and cards with the men's photographs and e-mail addresses. A slim Palestinian teenager serves us Arabic coffee. The three men emerge about 10 minutes later dressed in business suits, friendly but sombre. I'm a bit relieved to not have to translate. They all speak impeccable English. Muhammad Totah, the spokesman, thanks us for visiting and introduces his colleagues.

"Israel wants to deport us from Jerusalem, which is prohibited under Article 49 of the Fourth Geneva Convention," Totah informs us. "We are afraid *our* deportation order will open the doors to thousands of deportation orders. The International Committee of the Red Cross gave us a room to sleep in. Our families bring us food and clean clothes every day.

"Jimmy Carter came yesterday and heard our case. He witnessed the 2006 elections. The international community said it would respect the election results.

"The Change and Reform Party got 60 percent of the Palestinian vote. Four months after the elections, Israel arrested 64 elected members, most of them Ministers in the Palestinian Legislative Council.

"We have many political parties. Israel considers Hamas a terrorist organization. Has Hamas taken any action outside our land? Israel is accusing us of being disloyal to the state. How can we be disloyal to our occupier?" Totah asks. "It is understandable. Any occupied person will say they want to destroy the occupier.

"The world thinks this is a conflict between two countries, but that's not the reality. It is one country, an occupied land, an oppressed people. We don't have weapons. If Israel wants to take it all, it can. How can an oppressed people stand up against an army with nuclear weapons?"

We sit like silent statues. Jina shakes her head and cries. At one point, one of the men, Khaled Abu Arafeh, also the former Minister of Jerusalem Affairs, excuses himself to give an interview. It is painful to watch him, a diminutive man, standing inside the open gate, speaking into the camera, careful his toes do not extend even a millimetre outside the compound property. But I am also inspired. For the past 117 days, these men have met with visiting dignitaries from around the world, held press conferences and distributed information about their struggle.

"My five-year-old daughter asks why I am not at home like her cousin's father," Totah continues. "She thinks I don't love her. I failed. I don't know what to tell her. All of us are deprived of our families."

Muhammad Totah is a striking man, articulate and calm. It's difficult to look into his eyes.

"We have an enemy," he says. "Not the Jews. Our enemy is the Occupation. We respect all religions. Remove the Occupation and you remove the enemy. Our only demand is freedom. We are not criminals. I have a master's degree and I took part in the elections to practice democracy, despite the Occupation. We can't give anything without getting anything."

It's now twilight and there's a chill in the air. We take photographs with the men and our group walks back to Nablus Road where we say goodbye to Mariam and part ways. It's difficult to leave Jina.

"Thank you for translating for us," she says, as we hang on to one another, crying, kissing each other on the cheeks. It feels as if I am saying goodbye to my sister.

I look up and down Nablus Road. The darkness disorientates me.

Sensing this, David points the way. "I'll walk you to your hotel."

I'm grateful for his care and compassion. He waits while I gather my notebooks and walks with me to the Educational Bookstore. Reluctantly, I hand them over to the shop owner, praying they make it to my house in

Edmonton. He wraps them with the DVD and weighs the package. I pay the postage charge and retrieve my memory cards.

Almost a year later, I check some on-line news outlets to determine the status of the three Palestinian politicians. According to a June 10, 2011 report by *Nena News*, the three men are still at the Red Cross compound. They have been sequestered there for 345 days, "sleeping on the floor of an unused office and washing in a bathroom equipped with just a sink and toilet."

On January 23, 2012, after spending 569 days at the International Red Cross headquarters, the *Jerusalem Post* reported that Israel arrested the men and convicted them of belonging to a terrorist organization and illegally residing in Jerusalem.

TWENTY-ONE

Sleepless in Jerusalem

There I see you, Night, awful and beautiful, poised between heaven and earth, veiled in mist, cloaked in cloud, laughing at the sun, ridiculing the day, taunting the slaves who sleeplessly worship before the idols.

Kahlil Gibran, Thoughts and Meditations, *1993*

Emotionally spent, I heave my suitcases onto the bed and quickly empty them, organizing their contents into little mounds on the floor: clean clothes, dirty laundry, books, gifts and mementos. Accounts I heard from international peace activists about their treatment at Ben Gurion airport suddenly invade my thoughts. Detentions, confiscation of cameras, deportations, lengthy interrogations, some were even beaten and jailed. I'm gripped with fear about having to go through airport security tomorrow.

I tell myself, "You might get lucky again." When I departed from Ben Gurion airport near Tel Aviv last year, I was not interrogated and my bags were not searched, but a much louder voice inside me shoots back.

This time you might not be so lucky.

I decide to purge some of my mementoes. I sit cross-legged on the floor and begin ripping up a copy of the itinerary for the olive harvest, several pamphlets and a calendar produced by the Alternative Tourism Group.

"Shame on you," I say aloud, looking at the pile of paper in front of me, grateful no one can see me, except God and the four walls that envelope me.

I spot a trash can in the corner of the room and toss in the shredded paper.

I remember the invitation handed out during the sit-in at Sheikh Jarrah by members of the Palestinian Legislative Council and dig it out of my camera bag. The potential for being accused of collaborating with Hamas makes me shudder. My hands tremble as I tear the card into tiny pieces.

I feel as if I have done something criminal, as if just being who I am and who I associated with might become a problem. I've never felt such a cocktail of fear, helplessness and profound loneliness. I try to ignore my thoughts and repack my bags, placing the books at the bottom of the larger suitcase and covering them with stacks of folded clothes. I wrap a pair of pants, dusty and stained at the knees from picking olives, around my journal and I stuff them between layers of clothes, aware of the futility, knowing airport officials will be able to observe the contents of my bags when they pass through the x-ray machine or when they are inspected by hand.

I conceal my camera cards inside a sock and place it in the pocket of a fleece jacket. In case the cards are discovered, and airport officials insist on viewing my photographs, I decide to thwart their efforts by draining my camera battery. I sit at the edge of the bed and fire off the flash at the opposite wall. Not a clever idea. The white light bouncing back is blinding. I glance down at my camera and realize the battery is almost fully charged. It will take hours to deplete. I know I am being paranoid, but I worry, too, that someone walking past my window might notice the intermittent white light through the tiny slits in the shutters and think I am doing something I shouldn't. After a few minutes, I abandon the effort, remove the battery from the camera and bury it in my make-up bag.

The ring of the telephone makes me jump in my skin, highlighting the silence in the room. I look around, as if expecting someone to be standing there, remind myself I am safe and answer it. It is the front desk informing me that David is in the lobby waiting to see me. He had promised to come back after he ate his dinner. I meet him in the courtyard outside the lobby. I'm happy to see him.

"I wanted to make sure you are okay," he says like a concerned brother.

"Thanks. I'm just anxious about leaving tomorrow."

"You *are* taking a risk. You should have mailed your camera cards and journal," David reminds me, not meaning to add to my nervousness.

It dawns on me that if I am detained or arrested tomorrow, I doubt the Canadian government would come to my rescue, let alone even criticize Israeli policies and practices.

"There's a chance you won't be interrogated or searched," David adds, trying to help, but there is little conviction in his voice. We chat for a couple of minutes before he leaves, promising to stay in touch.

Back in my room, I am too anxious to sleep. I turn the television on and flick mindlessly through the channels. Oprah is on. The episode, with Arabic subtitles, is about people who suffer from schizophrenia, and I am reminded how being in the Holy Land has often felt schizophrenic.

I am still wide awake after watching several hours of television. Slumber remains as elusive as peace in the Holy Land, even following a long hot shower, which I thought might help me relax. Instead, I toss from side to side throughout the night, counting down the hours until dawn.

TWENTY-TWO

Smuggling Stories

When I came back from the West Bank to Bahrain I had in my suitcase about two kilos of Palestinian earth collected from one of the olive fields where we worked. I had also some beautiful stones, heavy to carry but sentimentally important to me. Now I have planted two olive trees in my garden and in the compost I mixed some of the Palestinian earth in a sort of symbolic gesture. This you may find childish but I want to believe that there will be a connection in this blend of earths and that the trees will bear beautiful fruits of peace.

Bertrand Espousy
E-mail to 2010 Olive Harvest Participants
February 17, 2011

Now I know how smugglers feel, trying to go through airport security. Only, my suitcases are not stuffed with drugs or other contraband. They are filled with stories. I'm smuggling out stories seldom, if ever, reported by mainstream media, stories Israel does not want you to read, stories from an occupied people.

I smoke half a cigarette before going inside the airport to take my place at the end of a line of people leading to an x-ray machine. I try to hide my anxiousness by relaxing my raised shoulders and taking slow, deep breaths through my nose. It does little to calm my jitters. I mentally rehearse the answers to potential questions I might be asked by airport officials, somewhat confident I will not raise suspicion with my "western" clothes and a face that fits in as one of the locals in many countries, a blend that includes, but is not limited to, Levantine Arabs, European Crusaders and conquering Mongols. I remind myself about the many times the locals here mistook me for being Jewish. And, I take some comfort in being able to hide my religious affiliation, if necessary. I am a Muslim, but detecting that would be daunting given I do not wear a *hijab*. I am not a walking stereotype or target. The terrorist attacks of 911 and one of the aftermaths, Islamophobia, make me think twice in some instances about admitting to be a Muslim.

I am more nervous at the prospect of having to lie about my activities in the Holy Land, of pretending to be an indifferent tourist, to avoid further questions and possible detention, or worse. I am simply incompetent at lying and would rather avoid it. Like most people, I was raised to believe lying is unethical and immoral. What has stuck with me since childhood is the notion that people, particularly my mother, can spot a lie.

My mind wanders as the long string of travellers edges closer to the x-ray machine. Suddenly, I'm six years old again, standing in front of my mother, looking up at her towering frame, answering her questions.

"You better be telling me the truth," she cautions. "I can *smell* if you are lying."

I believed her wholeheartedly. And here I am about to go through security at Ben Gurion, scheming to lie in likely the world's most sophisticated airport, whose trained personnel appreciate human behaviour and are skilled at detecting lies. In this moment, I just want to be home already, fearful I will pay for participating in the non-violent demonstration in Bil'in, for meeting with Hamas officials to hear their story of deportation and for the altercation with a settler in Sheikh Jarrah who tried to take my photograph.

"Are you travelling alone?" asks a loud female voice, seemingly out of nowhere. Startled, I turn around to face an airport security officer and quickly answer "yes."

"Your passport."

I hand it over. She flips through the navy-coloured booklet to the identification page, looks at my photograph then glances up at my face. She asks what the abbreviation "BRA" stands for. It is the country where I was born.

I respond politely, "Brazil."

So far, so good.

"How do you say your last name?"

She catches me unprepared for questions about my surname, the same infamous surname that has been associated with the terrorist attacks of 911. I pronounce the version I go by, which rhymes with Farrah, as in the late actress Farrah Fawcett.

"It's an Arabic name, pronounced *Jarrrah*," she says, rolling her "rs," enunciating the name clearly, all the while staring me in the eye.

I want to say, "And your question?" But I do not dare and manage only to mumble something about it being my married name, and that I am no longer married.

"Wait here," she orders.

My heart falls to the pit of my stomach. She tells the people lined up behind me to continue around and walks away with my passport. I remain in the same spot, looking straight ahead, trying to ignore the over-the-back stares of people as they walk past me pulling their suitcases. I wonder what they must be thinking. I've been lucky up until now. Many family members, including my children have experienced racial profiling at airports, but this is my first time. Now I know what racial profiling feels like. It is humiliating to be singled out.

A long five minutes later, the airport official returns.

"I need to ask you some questions," she says, stone-faced, and directs the people now lined up behind me to back up, seemingly for more privacy. When they do not move back fast enough she raises her voice using a combination of English and Hebrew. I try to appear unbothered despite my heart pounding wildly in my chest. I am certain she can hear it.

"What did you come here for?"

"I came as a tourist."

"Where did you go?"

"Jerusalem. Bethlehem. The Dead Sea."

"We think you might be carrying a bomb," she blurts out.

I freeze. Shocked, I do not respond and wonder for a second if I actually heard what I heard, aware that my mouth is open but no words are escaping. I rationalize that I have nothing to fear. I know I am not carrying a bomb, still the tops of my ears burn, my legs tremble like jelly and my breath is jagged at the uncertainty of what might happen next. I try focusing on the barrage of questions that follow, certain she can sense my nervousness and knows I am hiding something.

"Did you stay with any local family?"

"No."

"Where did you stay?"

"At a hotel."

"Who did you meet?"

"Friends."

"Where are they from?"

"England."

"What are their names?"

I mention Jeni, Paul and David, the first names that pop into my head, since I spent the last day in Sheikh Jarrah with them. She pauses. I'm thankful she does not press further for their surnames, which elude me. My thoughts turn to my bags, which tell the story of my actual activities in the Holy Land: three camera cards capturing the reality on the ground in the Occupied Palestinian Territories, the olive harvest, the sit-ins and the demonstration in Bil'in, my journal, a number of books and brochures about the occupation of Palestine and mementos from the olive harvest that I just could not jettison last night and risked bringing with me.

The lunacy of it all hits me. I am not guilty of smuggling a bomb, illegal drugs or other contraband. I am certain what I am doing is not illegal, even under Israeli law. My aim is simply to convey the stories about the true victims, stories the State of Israel wants to keep hidden about the reality in the Holy Land, and it has the power to make my exit difficult, detain me. I do not want to bring worry to my elderly parents and my children who are expecting me to be home at a certain time.

The security officer turns her attention to my bags by placing stickers imprinted with a certain alpha-numeric code. I assume to distinguish them for the baggage handlers behind the scenes.

"Follow me," she says when she finishes and leads me to the mouth of a large x-ray machine.

"Place your bags here," she points.

I hoist them onto the conveyor belt. It spits them out one at a time through a large opening at the opposite end where I retrieve them, and she escorts me to a nearby area. Two young, female security guards clutch wands tipped with white gauze-like strips, waiting to inspect my two suitcases and camera bag. I place my bags onto the stainless steel inspection table as directed.

"Open them."

I unzip the bags. The women take a bag each, emptying clothes and books, meticulously feeling in between items and scanning for explosives. I wait as they inspect every inch of my bags, and assume they will also search me to see if I have a bomb hidden under my clothes. I expect a pat-down or strip-down at best and an orifice inspection at worst.

But none of that happens. Neither of them is interested in the contents of my camera cards, journal or books.

"Okay. You can close your bags," one of the women finally says, after what seems like 15 minutes. She helps me re-pack. I care little about reorganizing my things and place them haphazardly, trying not to appear too eager.

"Have a good flight," she tells me.

I will now, I think as I walk towards several lines at the check-in area, praying the worst is over. As I wait my turn in the queues, I wonder what it was that compelled airport officials to suspect I was carrying a bomb. If they were actually concerned about a bomb, why did they not check my shoes or under my clothes?

Was it simply my Arabic surname? Were they playing me, a mere, middle-age peace activist?

I will never know.

The ordeal leaves me famished. After checking in I find the food court and buy a kosher McChicken at a McDonalds. I still have a two-hour wait for my 12-hour flight to Toronto, but decide to head over to my departure gate and eat there. All the while, I assume cameras are recording my every step. I start thinking that, at any second, an Israeli police officer or soldier in civilian clothes is going to pull me aside and interrogate me further. When I reach my departure lounge, I plop myself down in one of the chairs, unwrap my burger and eat.

I spot Bertrand, one of the volunteer olive pickers, as he is walking by. He notices me, strides over and takes a seat beside me.

"Nice to see you again!" we both say in unison. I feel a sense of relief seeing his kind, familiar face.

"What did you do on your last day?" I ask.

"Wandered about in Bethlehem. And you?"

"I went back to Sheikh Jarrah with several of the olive pickers from England," I tell him. "We met with elected members of the Palestine Legislative Council. You probably heard about them. Israel is trying to deport them from Jerusalem."

He nods.

"I read about them."

I break down when I share my experience going through Israeli security. He listens sympathetically.

"I'm sorry you went through that."

I notice his eyes becoming misty. I'm touched and feel privileged to have formed this and other lasting friendships in the Holy Land, aware the experience over the past two weeks has brought the olive pickers closer together and strengthened our resolve when we return home to continue, in our own way, to work for peace and an end to Israel's military occupation of the Palestinians — to "keep hope alive."

At about 20,000 feet above sea level, the pilot announces that all passengers must remain seated with their seatbelts fastened, until we clear Israeli air space. It is a military command. Even up here is the same prison-like feeling I endured the entire time I was in the Occupied Palestinian Territories. I am relieved to be heading home. Away from a world of walls, watchtowers and checkpoints. Away from a world of house demolitions, forced evictions and child imprisonments. Away from a place where thousand-year-old olive trees are toppled to build illegal Jewish settlements and swimming pools. Away from the relentless oppression, violence and omnipresent, armed soldiers. I have seen things that will haunt me forever. The Holy Land is a frightening place. Its hills and *wadis*, its water resources, its historic and religious sites, its people, their dreams and livelihoods, even its plants—are all under siege. In this moment, I do not wish to return any time soon, and it hurts. I feel weak for barely persevering a mere two weeks of what the Palestinians have endured for decades. I am on my way home, free, but I leave behind Palestinians who remain dispossessed and imprisoned behind walls.

As our west-bound jet soars above the Mediterranean Sea at cruising altitude, the pilot soon switches off the seatbelt sign. I settle comfortably into my seat.

"*Alhamdulillah*. Thank you, God," I say to myself. "I made it out safely with my suitcases of smuggled stories."

TWENTY-THREE

O Little Town
of Bethlehem

The road to the other side of Israel is not signposted. It is a place
you rarely read about in your newspapers or hear about from your
television sets. It is all but invisible to most Israelis.
Susan Nathan, The Other Side of Israel:
My Journey Across the Jewish/Arab Divide, *2005*

I am here but not here. Physically I am in Canada, but my heart hovers
over the Holy Land, in particular Bethlehem and its surrounding hills.
The khaki-coloured pants that I wore picking olives still sit on a chair in
my bedroom, unwashed, smudged at the knees with the red earth of Palestine
and splotched with hallowed oil from its olive trees. I unfold them, bury my
face in them and inhale. They still smell like Palestine. I cannot bring myself
to wash them, so I tuck them into the bottom of a drawer.

I am relieved to be home, away from the violence. And, at the same time,
I feel guilty for being back in my secure and peaceful surroundings, back to
my unfettered, comfortable life, while the Palestinians remain dispossessed
and subjugated, enduring a hellish existence. I go through the motions at
work; the issues surrounding wildfire management, while crucial, now seem
minor by comparison to the reality in the Occupied Palestinian Territories.

Sumud's last words, *khaleekee salbee,* "stay strong," when we parted,
continue to swirl in my head. I still hear Safi reciting Arabic poetry. And,

on Fridays, a day of communal prayer and protests in villages throughout the Occupied Palestinian Territories, I think about the residents of Bil'in, especially Rani, leading the demonstration in his wheelchair. I picture him through white clouds of tear gas, taking photographs, refusing to give up fighting for his land, for equality and peace.

Friends and co-workers ask, "How was your holiday?"

They genuinely want to know, but I am stumped as to where to start. I mention it was hardly a holiday and share snippets of my smuggled stories. They listen respectfully and look back at me, doe-eyed in disbelief. I do not fault them; many are unaware of the truth about the Israeli-Palestinian "conflict," largely because western corporate media continues to feed unsuspecting viewers misinformation, too little information or outright lies and propaganda, which serves to perpetuate the many myths and hide the facts. Some people I know actually believe it is the Palestinians who are occupying Israel, not the other way around. I take the time to describe life for Palestinians and mention some of my activities.

"You crrayzee?" my mother asks in her thick accent when I share my experience. Other family members shake their heads disapprovingly and have difficulty appreciating why I would intentionally put myself in harm's way. I am not sure I totally appreciate why myself. I was driven by a profound need to help somehow, to show my solidarity with the oppressed, to act rather than simmer in silence.

I reminisce about my first journey with the Arab Jewish Women's Peace Coalition, comparing it to my recent adventures picking olives for Palestinians, which brought me closer to the "conflict." The first trip was an incredible learning and bonding experience, and I would not trade it for anything, but I felt more like a voyeur, observing the place largely from the outside, looking in; it left me wanting more.

"Tell the people in Canada about us. Put pressure on your government to stop ignoring our suffering," which I heard often, constantly rings in my ear. I hurry home, where I sequester myself in the evenings and on weekends, writing feverishly about my experiences, the people I met, the stories I heard, the places I visited. I function on five hours of restless sleep a night. An inexplicable energy drives me and I wake up at the break of dawn every morning, refreshed.

Traumatized by the daily violence I had just witnessed in the Holy Land, I vowed not to return there any time soon when I first arrived home. Now, only two weeks later, I am aching to go back.

That feeling becomes more intense as Christmas approaches. For the first time in my life, I feel the need to celebrate the birth of Jesus in Bethlehem. I want to experience Christmas in front of the Church of Nativity with some of the many Palestinians I was lucky to meet. By late November, the City of Edmonton is aglow with lights. Winking streamers of different colours hang from homes and trees. Shopping malls are transformed, too. Giant Christmas trees draped in ornaments and tinsel stand like sentinels beside replicas of the Nativity Scene. Store shelves brim with decorations and wrapping paper, toys and trinkets, enticing shoppers with a plethora of gift ideas.

Christmas is a contemplative and wonderful time of year, even for people who might not have Jesus or his birthplace on their minds. All the glitz and glitter is uplifting, but a part of me grieves for the Bethlehem I witnessed only two months ago. The "Little Town of Bethlehem" is under military siege, surrounded by prison-like walls, parts of it rendered into ghettos as "silent stars go by."

About a week before Christmas, Dr. Elizabeth Ordonez, one of the olive pickers, sends an e-mail to the 2010 olive harvest participants. She, too, appears to have Bethlehem on her mind and shares with us her thought-provoking, "revised" version of the popular Christmas carol, *O Little Town of Bethlehem*:

> Oh, little Town of Bethlehem,
> how trapped we see thee lie;
> above thy grieved and restless sleep
> the mournful stars go by.
> For in thy dark streets lurketh
> the everlasting might;
> the raids and fears of all the years
> may still occur tonight.

For you are still surrounded
by walls and guns and hate,
so while you sleep, the soldiers keep
their guard and seal the gate.
O morning brings the struggle
to pass checkpoints again,
to build another settlement
that robs from you and kin.

How silently, how silently,
the world averts its eyes;
too passively accepts the force
of occupation's lies.
Few ears have heard its coming,
for in this world of din,
the meek souls all around the world
too easily let it in.

Oh, stalwart soul of Bethlehem,
keep hope alive, we pray;
cast out the thieves, take back your land,
be born again today!
We hear the choir of justice
the hopeful tidings tell;
O, come freedom, abide with us,
release us from this hell!

Her poem resonates with me, as I imagine it does with the other olive pickers. We witnessed the theft of Palestinian homes and lands, pubescent looking soldiers enforcing the military occupation and colonization of Palestinian territory by manning walls, watchtowers, and checkpoints surrounding Bethlehem. We all heard countless stories of house demolitions and evictions, child imprisonments, women denied entry and giving birth at checkpoints, and other incidents of settler and soldier violence against Palestinians.

Dr. Ordonez's poem also offers hope, triggers a longing for the innocence of ignorance, when I was in grade one at Vera M Welsh Elementary school in Lac La Biche. That was where I learned to sing "O Little Town of Bethlehem" for the first time, imagining a mythical place, sensing it was holy without knowing what holy meant, without knowing I would one day visit Bethlehem.

But, the biblical Bethlehem I once imagined and sang about no longer exists.

I google "O Little Town of Bethlehem" and discover an American priest, who became enamoured by the hills surrounding Bethlehem during a pilgrimage, wrote this classic Christmas carol in 1868. I wonder how different the author's words would be if he witnessed the holy city today.

Christmas morning, the aroma of freshly brewed coffee and blueberry pancakes floats into my room, entices me to get out of bed. I'm in Lac La Biche. My older sister, who lives here, invited me to spend the holidays with her. I eat breakfast and watch as she prepares stuffing for the duck she plans on roasting.

Later, I turn on her television, hoping to catch a glimpse of the prayers and celebrations in Bethlehem. The *BBC News* shows a short clip of Palestinians, both Muslim and Christian, mingling around a giant Christmas tree in Manger Square. The desire to be there with them is intense. I cannot explain it; I was not raised to celebrate Christmas, and I am not necessarily "religious," but, as a Muslim, I was taught to revere Jesus. I believe Jesus was special. The Qur'an elaborates about Jesus's miraculous birth, and there are more references to Virgin Mary and Jesus than the Prophet Mohammed, peace be upon them all.

"I wish I could be there," I think out loud.

My sister, who is relaxing on the sofa across from me, flashes me a look of incredulity without responding.

As 2009 winds down, Safi's friend sends me a short e-mail informing me that Israel has once again imprisoned Safi. The news hits me like a punch in my stomach, and for days I picture Safi tied up in a contorted position, Israeli soldiers beating him, denying him sleep and food, and Safi holding back tears. I can't shake these images from my head. I dream about standing in front of a prison, in the hot sun somewhere in a desert, begging soldiers to release Safi, threatening not to leave until they let him go. I wake up with the soldiers' laughter ringing in my ears.

On New Years Eve, as millions of North Americans congregate to usher in 2011, I am again watching a *BBC News* report about a mother in Bil'in, who is mourning the death of her middle-aged daughter, Jawaher. I jump to my feet the second I recognize the familiar hills on the outskirts of Bil'in in the short news clip. Jawaher was killed by inhaling tear gas, which Israeli soldiers fired at her and other protestors at Friday's demonstration earlier in the day. The Israeli army denies responsibility for her death and alleges she died of cancer. My heart aches for Jawaher's mother. Two years prior, she also lost a son, Bassam. He was directly hit with a tear gas canister in the chest, also at a Friday demonstration. I cannot imagine losing a child, let alone two. As a mother, I wonder if she still thinks the protests are worth it. How does she cope with the realization that in all likelihood, there will be no justice for Jawaher? It is a terrible irony for someone whose name means, "precious gem."

Less than a year after volunteering for the olive harvest, I am again waiting to board a flight to Tel Aviv at Pearson airport in Toronto. This time I am returning to the Holy Land as an actual "pilgrim."

I am part of a Canadian delegation of Jews, Christians and Muslims, who signed up for a first-of-its-kind tour entitled, "In the Path of Abraham." It is an opportunity to visit the various religious sites and holy places for each group, even though I visited some of the sites before. It is a chance to see more of the places I read about in the Bible, to walk where Jesus is said to have walked, to stand on Sermon Mount where he preached, to visit the cave where he cured the lepers. It is a chance to offer prayers in the Garden of Gethsemane in the shade of olive trees thousands of years old, to pray at the base of the Western Wall and in the Al-Aqsa mosque. It is also a chance to visit Safi's family and others in the Bethlehem district, whom I had the privilege of meeting and would love to see again. It is a chance to smuggle out more stories.

Out of the 50 of us who joined the Path of Abraham tour, led by a rabbi, an imam, a reverend and a catholic priest, it is hard to ignore the fact that only the Muslims in our group are being singled out for interrogation by EL AL airlines staff at the boarding gate. They instruct us to sit off to one side of the waiting area. A pleasant young man asks me a series of questions about my previous visits and I respond with half-truths. He takes my camera bag somewhere for closer inspection. As I wait for him to return with it, I watch as, one by one, the other Muslim women, of various ages, who are all wearing a *hijab*, and one, a convert from Guatemala, who wears a *niqab*, a face covering, are escorted behind a portable black screen by female personnel. While I am grateful for the security and for being spared from showing my nakedness to a stranger behind a screen, I did not expect to be subjected to religious profiling while still on Canadian soil. I know, however, that this indignity pales in comparison to the daily humiliations faced by Palestinians in the Holy Land.

Hours later, somewhere over the Atlantic Sea, as our plane slices through the frigid black firmament high above the clouds, passengers around me are enjoying the bliss of sleep while I am wide-awake, musing about my destiny, grateful I have some control over it. I am on my way back to the Holy Land with the widest smile on my face — *another wondrous journey of learning awaits me.*

Acknowledgements

This book would not have been possible without the many Israelis and Palestinians I had the privilege of meeting and the Palestinian families I temporarily lived with during my travels in the Holy Land, peace builders who graciously and generously shared their stories, enlightened and inspired me with their wisdom, who showed me what courage, resiliency, non-violent resistance and "keeping hope alive" look like.

I am indebted to my former teacher, Scot Morison, and classmates at MacEwan University's 2009/2010 Publishing Prose class, who work-shopped several first-draft chapters for this book, and provided encouragement and expressed interest in the subject matter, the need to tell these stories that they "never hear on the evening news." And to Sophie Lees, my former teacher at MacEwan University, for helping me to believe I can.

I am also indebted to the following coworkers, friends and family members, who in the beginning of the writing process read a few of the chapters and offered valuable opinions, namely: Dr. Jumana Jarrah, Janan Jarrah, Anwar Jarrah, Jamila Fyith Simon, Nancy Hamoud, Omar Zaitoun, Iman Zaitoun, Joseph Gudz, Amanda Bereska, Neal McLoughlin, Hua Sun, Jules LeBoeuf, Charlene Albert Guerin, Tracey Bidne, Goldwin McEwan, Dr. Katherine MacLean, Professor Margaret McCallum, Faculty of Law, University of New Brunswick, fellow volunteer olive pickers and peace activists Sabah Fizazi and

Bertrand Espouy and Kristel in the Occupied Palestinian Territories.

Thank you to Nahida in Exile and Dr. Elizabeth Ordonez for allowing me to quote their poems.

My deepest gratitude to my three editors: Ellen Kartz, Khalid Taha and Susan Giffin.

I thank my children for telling me they are proud of me. It helped to know. In particular, thank you to my son for suggesting the book's title.

Ultimately, I am most indebted to God…

And, to my parents: my 91-year-old father, a male Scheherazade, who mesmerized me as a child with fables from the homeland, beginning each story with *Kan ya ma kan*, "There was and there was not." Thank you for teaching me the power of the *word*. Mostly, I am grateful you were brave enough to leave behind your home, twice immigrating to new continents, practically penniless, without the security of an education or trade, learning new languages and customs. How fortunate for me we ended up in Canada, growing up in the small town of Lac La Biche amid Nature's splendour, in peace. And, thank you to my number one hero, my precocious 87-year-old mother, who still has a memory like a computer, speaks Arabic, Portuguese and English, but is illiterate. Born in a time, circumstance and place where families could only afford to send their boys to school, she continues to wish she had that opportunity. Thank you for planting in me the seeds of seeking knowledge, honesty and humility.

Selected Bibliography

Abuelaish, Dr. Izzeldin, 2010. *I Shall Not Hate: A Gaza Doctor's Journey.* Canada: Random House.

Abunimah, Ali, 2006. *One Country: A Bold Proposal to End the Israeli-Palestinian Impasse.* New York: Metropolitan Books.

Baltzer, Anna, 2007. *Witness in Palestine: A Jewish American Woman in the Occupied Territories.* Boulder, CO: Paradigm Publishers.

Barghouti, Mourid, 2000. *I Saw Ramallah.* Toronto: Random House of Canada Ltd.

Christison, Kathleen and Bill, 2009. *Palestine in Pieces: Graphic Perspectives on the Israeli Occupation.* New York: Pluto Press.

Keefer, Michael, 2010. *Antisemitism Real and Imagined: Oslo and After.* Toronto: Pandora Press.

LeBor, Adam, 2007. *City of Oranges: An Intimate History of Arabs and Jews in Jaffa.* New York: W. W. Norton & Company.

Luyendijk, Joris, 2009. *People Like Us: Misrepresenting the Middle East.* California: Soft Skull Press.

McGowan, Daniel and Ellis, Marc H., 1998. *Remembering Deir Yassin: The Future of Israel and Palestine.* New York: Olive Branch Press.

Nusseibeh, Sari with Anthony David, 2007. *Once Upon a Country: A Palestinian Life.* New York: Farrar, Straus and Giroux.

Pappe, Ilan, 2006. *The Ethnic Cleansing of Palestine*. Oxford: One World.

Peled, Miko, 2012. *The General's Son: Journey of an Israeli in Palestine*. Just World Publishing.

Sacco, Joe, 2008. *Palestine*. Seattle, WA: Fantagraphics Books.

Salem, Salwa, with Laura Maritano. 2007. *The Wind in My Hair*. Massachusetts: Interlink Publishing.

Shehadeh, Raja, 2002. *Strangers in the House: Coming of Age in Occupied Palestine*. London: Penguin Books.

Shihab, Aziz, 2007. *Does the Land Remember Me?: A Memoir of Palestine*. New York: Syracuse University Press.

Williams, Emma, 2010. *It's Easier to Reach Heaven Than the End of the Street: A Jerusalem Memoir*. Massachusetts: Interlink Publishing Group.

CPSIA information can be obtained at www.ICGtesting.com
Printed in the USA
LVOW08s0736090315

429741LV00001B/14/P